REDEEMED
A Journey from Darkness to Light

REDEEMED
A Journey from Darkness to Light

A Memoir of Extraordinary Lives

By
Bianella Orozco-DeLaHoz & Alain Orozco

BookGo

Copyright © 2025 by Bianella Orozco-DeLaHoz & Alain Orozco

All rights reserved. No part of this book may be reproduced in any manner whatsoever without written permission except in the case of brief quotations embodied in critical articles and reviews.

All photos in this book, on the jacket cover and case, are the property of the authors, Bianella Orozco-DeLaHoz and Alain Orozco. Any use of these photos, or copying them, is prohibited without the authors express permission.

All inquiries should be addressed to BookGo at www.bookgo.pub

Cover Design by Khadijah Ali

First Printing 2025

To my mother, Maria Isabel: your love and compassion continue to live through us, Nella and Alain, and your grandkids Isabella Maria, Dassio Adean, Bianella Isabel, Alanna Isabelle, Nina Marie and our future generations. "Mami, I kept my promise to never forget who makes the rainbow."

~ Nella

I dedicate this book first to our Lord and Savior and may the readers of this book know that you are the way and the light.

To my wife Ivette, my greatest love, you inspire me to be a better man. I am grateful for our love and for the life we built together.

To my daughters, the light of my life. This book is my way of sharing my struggles and lessons I have learned and how I was able to overcome adversity thanks to God. May it inspire you, know that with a relationship with God you can overcome all obstacles in your lives. My life is complete because of you girls.

To my sister, Nella who has shared with me all these tragic events. I am proud of the woman you have become and of the beautiful family you have created. To those who read this book I pray you find inspiration and know anything is possible and that you are not alone.

~ Alain

This book is a memoir of our lives from childhood to now. We have tried to recreate events, locales, and conversations from our memories of them. Some conversations have been recreated and/or supplemented, and the details of some individuals have been changed to respect their privacy. We hope you are inspired by our story.

~ Nella and Alain

INTRODUCTION

The book is in two voices because we are two people telling the same story, but from the perspective of how we saw it. We were both there, but we looked at things through different eyes, and so, you will hear us tell you in our own voices what happened.

Rather, you will hear what we lived. This book is the story of our extraordinary life, so far. We are twins, and our twinship has been essential to how we have managed to get through what we did, and to come out as successful, healthy people. Without each other, we don't know if we could have managed it, and thankfully, we won't have to know because we were always there to support each other in both terrible and good times.

Even if we weren't there physically, in the same room, due to events that you shall discover in our story, we were there emotionally and spiritually, knowing that even though we might be alone in a room, we were never truly alone because the other was there with us, in our heart.

So as you read our story, we ask you to bear in mind that, even though we are twins, we are two different people, and we will see things differently. It's a bit like that wonderful film Rashomon, in which the same crime story is told seven different ways as it explores the philosophy of justice. We are not trying to tell our story through many different lenses, but there will be times when one of us sees or feels something that the other didn't. And you will notice.

Like Rashomon, ours too is a story of terrible crime and eventual justice. It was through our own lives, through our epic struggles and our sometimes unexpected triumphs, that we got not only justice for ourselves, but we found redemption. We hope that our story inspires you to look into your own lives with a new perspective, and to see things that you might not have seen before. We are not alone, for we have God who loves us immensely and wants the best for us even when things may be falling apart around us. In that way, you too may find a path from the darkness into the light.

CHAPTER 1: June 9, 1982

It was the last week of school for us, and we should have been happy that summer joys was just around the corner. Except that joy was very much not around the corner. And what happened on that day changed everything, forever. For the worse, and then, for the better. This is how it happened.

Alain remembers...
It was June 9, 1982. My sister Bianella, whom we call Nella, and I attended the Perrine Baptist Academy, a Christian school in Perrine, a suburb of Miami, Florida. The city was undergoing a transformation from a retirement destination to a cultural one, with renovated hotels popping up, and a lively music scene, all combined with intense drug battles, as the Medellin cartel was in town and doing business. But all we knew at the time was that we were going to be graduating from the fifth to the sixth grade in a week or so, and we were excited to move up in the world. We were especially excited because on the morning of June 9, we were scheduled to go on a field trip to the Sunshine Roller Skating Rink.

Roller skating was a thing back in the 1980s, and it was my thing. I loved it. I used to go skating every weekend, and as an eleven-year-old boy, I was eager to show off my skating skills to my classmates. I was an athletic kid who loved football. To look at me, I was your average Hispanic

American kid with dark hair and light brown eyes. I'm normally light skinned, but my sister and I, we sucked up the sun as much as possible. And in Miami there's a lot of sunshine.

Our uncle, Francisco Gomez, whom we called Kiko, was at our house on that warm June morning. He was our mother's older brother, and he had been living with us for the past month. He was tall and lean and had dark curly hair and olive skin. He was a lovely man. He had a great energy to him, and he was funny. My sister and I loved him.

Our mother's family in Colombia is one you could call middle class; they had car repair shops and trucking companies, but even the middle class is not rich there compared to the United States. Her family was close. Our mother was the youngest of six brothers and sisters. Her sister Luz was the oldest, then her sister Nubia, her brother Guillermo who we called "Memo", and then Kiko. They had a third brother John, who was murdered six months before we were born. Violence was always circling around my family, here and in Colombia.

Kiko also had a dark past. He had been arrested back in 1978 for possession of eighteen kilos of cocaine in Miami-Dade County. He spent about six months in Miami-Dade County Jail. When he finally got bailed out, he escaped back to Colombia. He never faced US time for the crime.

In 1982, he came back to the US via Mexico. He had been a trucker in Medellin, Colombia, driving a 10-ton dump truck. But he wanted to come back and work with his sister, my mother, in the drug business because his wife was pregnant with their fourth child and he wanted to make extra money. This would then allow him to go back to Colombia and build his trucking business and do better for his growing family.

So he showed up at our house about a month before our roller skating field trip. My father owned two Texaco gas stations in Miami, one of them on Le Jeune and Flagler, close to the Miami Airport, and another one a couple of miles away on 16th and Coral Way. One of them was called Orozco's Texaco. The other one was called Zapata's Texaco. However, our father's main business was dealing drugs, and Kiko was getting into the drug business with our father.

On that June morning in 1982, Kiko was driving my sister and me to school in my mother's white Corvette. As we were about to leave, our mother came out of the house to say goodbye to us. I remember her wearing a long white nightgown. She said goodbye to us as she made the sign of the cross over us, which she always did. My mother was raised Catholic and would bring us to church on Sundays–like it or not. My mother knew I was looking forward to skating on our field trip that day. She would take me to the Kendall Skating Center every Saturday morning for two sessions of skating. I was very spoiled by my mother, a huge contrast from our earlier days on welfare in Brooklyn where toys were scarce. Since moving to Miami in 1977, we went from a small apartment to a modest house; to opulent houses with pools and maids; from public to private school, and from playing with a box of mismatched toys to having expensive speed skates, motorcycles and video games at our disposal.

My mother loved both of us very much, and she was very close to my sister. They were joined at the hip. I was a little wilder and my mother worried about me a lot. I had already broken my arms four times: in Brooklyn, in Colombia, then twice in Miami, and so I was always going in and out of the hospital. I almost died when I was eight in a horseback riding accident in Colombia. I fell off a horse, cracked my skull, and had internal bleeding. My mother was always looking out for me, telling me to be careful.

So, that day, Kiko drove us off to school and dropped my sister and me off in the driveway of the Perrine Baptist Academy. And then we went off on our rolling skating field trip.

Nella remembers...
The night before the roller skating field trip, I was getting ready for it at home. I asked my mom if she could help me iron my jeans. I liked everything just right. I was always a careful person. I was petite in frame with olive skin. Dark brown, curly, frizzy hair. I was very shy and quiet but smiled a lot. I've always had a beautiful smile. My eyes and smile are a true expression of my soul. I was not encouraged to speak my mind or to reveal my emotions; my father thought

it was disrespectful for a girl to reveal too much. Although quiet, I was deep in thought with questions. My very first books were Cinderella and the Bible, which I believe inspired me with hopes of finding both love and God. Observing life in silence sharpened my skills at detecting others' emotions: anger, happiness, love—and also cruelty.

My mother was born in Medellin, Colombia and her name was Maria de Los Angeles. However, she had changed her name when she came to the United States and decided to call herself Maria Isabel, but everybody called her Maruja. I called her Mami.

So when I asked Mami to help iron my jeans, she said to me, "Well, you really have to learn how to do it. What if I die tomorrow? You have to learn how to do these things yourself."

I never forgot those words because they came true, and I did have to learn so much more without her. Whenever I am ironing or making a bed, I always think about what she said to me on her last night on earth. That last night was, ironically, very special because of my uncle Kiko, who I loved so much.

He was my favorite uncle, and he and my mom were very close. I felt so much love from him. He also made me feel very pretty. He would sing to me a song from Nat King Cole "*Yo vendo unos ojos negros*" (it means "I sell black eyes") with a loving smile. Indeed, he was the first man for whom I ever felt love. I would simply be walking through the hallway, and he would look at me and say, "Who is that beautiful girl? Look at those eyes!" He just made me feel so happy and he gave me the best hugs. He made me feel loved, not only as a niece, but as a daughter as well. I just adored him in a way that I did not adore my father. I was afraid of my father. He was very stern and angry. I had already witnessed his fury when he was beating my mother and us. His belts, his fists, his pulling of hair created a fear of him that he misread as respect.

So on that night before the roller skating trip, my mother, Kiko and I were all sitting at the kitchen counter. I don't know what we were talking about. But we were all laughing, and I was happy to have my mother and my uncle there. Then I went to bed and fell asleep. And I had a nightmare.

I dreamed of two tornadoes coming for us at school. I woke up very scared, and my mother rushed to my room. I told my mom that I had a terrible dream that frightened me. These terrifying tornadoes were coming after us and it was horrible. She calmed me down and reassured me that it was just something working itself out in my mind and that I would be fine.

As I got ready to leave for school, I asked my mother for money for the field trip and she went and got some for me. She was in her white nightgown. My brother was waiting in the car with my uncle to take us to school. I walked to the car, then turned and ran back to look back at my mother. She always gave us the Sign of the Cross blessing: "In the name of the Father, the Son and the Holy Spirit, and may the Virgin Mary accompany you." That's what she did on this day as well.

I got in the car and waved goodbye to my mother, not knowing it was my last time seeing her alive. As Uncle Kiko drove us to school, I remember just staring at his feet as he drove. Not too much later, I would see them on the TV news, sticking out from a white sheet as he lay on our front lawn . I don't know why I looked at them, but I did.

Once at school, with attendance taken, we got on a bus to go to the skating rink. I suddenly got a really bad stomach ache and went to the skating center to tell them that I wasn't feeling well. I called my mother from the skating center. There was no answer.

Alain remembers…

Later, what I found out was that on that morning, my father had gone to work and was at one of the Texaco gas stations he owned in Miami.

My father was a good-looking 45-year-old with jet black hair. He stood 5 feet 7 inches and weighed approximately 180 pounds. He presented himself as a very serious man, the oldest of six brothers and sisters, from an impoverished family out of the mining town of Amaga, an hour outside of Medellin, Colombia. He was good to his friends, and he was also a womanizer. He had a swagger to him, with a kind of mob look, and he was also very short tempered. He was physically abusive to the women he was with, whether it was a girlfriend or my mother. Same thing with the kids, as he certainly beat us. My cousin Alan shared with me that he was physically abusive with him as well. He told me about one time when my father got upset because my cousin came in and was jumping around the room. My father just picked him up by the hair and threw him across the room. The kids were crying and everybody was afraid of my father.

So on that day at the gas station, my father got a phone call from my mother saying, "El Monje is coming over." El Monje means "The Monk"; his sister Emma was called La Monja, "The Nun". My father told me she was given that nickname because she had wanted to be a nun at some point in her life. Her brother Fernando was nicknamed El Monje simply because of his sister. They were in their early thirties, about the same age as our mother. They were coming over to pay a debt owed from a previous drug deal. At the time, all I knew of my father's business was that he owned two Texaco gas stations in Miami and five video stores in Medellin, Colombia. On a couple of occasions I saw piles of cocaine lying on a table in our house which was explained to me as being flour for making cakes for a new bakery in Colombia. I knew something wasn't right with all these shady people that would come and go at the house. Especially after all the events that transpired prior to June 9, 1982.

Usually payment to my father would come in large bundles of money, especially because back then, a kilo of cocaine was very expensive. Its wholesale value was about $40-50,000 a kilo. My father told me they had been waiting on that three million dollar payment for weeks, and a few weeks earlier El Monje had shown up with less than $75,000.

So Fernando, El Monje, called asking if my father was home, and our mother had responded that he was, even though he wasn't, not knowing that Fernando had been calling from Old Cutler Hammock Park, which was literally around the corner from our house. The park is now called Bill Sadowski Park, after the congressman. The neighborhood we lived in was Perrine, which has since been renamed Palmetto Bay. It was upper class and predominantly white back then.

At the time of this phone call, my mother asked my uncle to change his clothes because they were having people over and he had been outside mowing the lawn. We had a big house on a cul-de-sac with four homes on it, and we had nice gardens and grounds. Kiko was helping to look after them.

Also in the house was our maid, Gloria. She was a very thin lady with black hair. I remember she read Spanish Tarot cards. Our mother was very religious, but she was also involved in the world of Tarot. About a month before the terrible events of that day, my aunt Lucero and her husband came to visit. She was my father's sister, in her mid-thirties. Her husband, Alberto, was one of the managers at my father's gas stations. We were in the kitchen of our house, and my sister was there as well. Gloria the maid was reading the Tarot cards to my mother, Aunt Lucero and Uncle Alberto.

When Gloria was reading the Tarot cards to Lucero, the death card came out. In that deck and in most Tarot cards, Death is shown in the card as a giant skeleton and takes the fateful number thirteen. Nella and I heard Gloria say, "This card says somebody's gonna die." My aunt and uncle asked, "Who?" Gloria didn't answer. And then she read the cards to my mother, and the death card came out again. They were trying to figure out who was going to die. Very soon they would have their answer.

Gloria was in our house when the men looking to pay the drug debt arrived and rang our doorbell that morning in June. My uncle was still getting dressed and was holding a shirt in his hands; this was confirmed by Gloria because she could see him from the kitchen, where she was standing. She heard him open the door and invite them to come in. They walked into the house and began shooting at Uncle Kiko with silenced guns.

My mother had been getting dressed herself when she stepped out of her bedroom to see who had arrived, only to see men shooting at her brother in the foyer. As she ran back into the bedroom one of the shooters chased her down, and Gloria heard my Uncle Kiko say, "No la maten a ella." Don't kill her.

One of the men continued to shoot Kiko as my uncle staggered backwards and tried to escape through the garage.

Kiko was pressing his body against the garage door to prevent the shooter from entering the garage, so the killer shot through the garage door five times, hitting Kiko again. Even so, Kiko was able to press the button to open the garage door onto the driveway, and he managed to make his way to the end of our driveway, finally collapsing on our lawn, on the grass he had just cut. The killers shot him a couple more times in the face. The police said he had been shot more than 50 times.

The fact that the killers were chasing our uncle and our mother and shooting them gave Gloria the maid time to hide in our father's office behind his desk, which ultimately saved her life. She later told us that she could see that the master bedroom doors were closed, which made her think our mother was inside the bedroom hiding and hearing the assassins pacing through the house.

Gloria waited fifteen minutes or so and then called my father at the gas station to tell him that something horrible had happened, not knowing that the police were already on their way. One of our neighbors had seen our uncle lying in a pool of blood and made the call to the police anonymously.

When the police arrived, they found Kiko lying dead outside. Gloria was in the house and our mother, who had been shot several times in the face, across her cheek and up to her ear, was found lying on the blue carpet floor at the entrance of her master bedroom. Gloria had not seen the killer go inside and murder our mother, then leave and close the bedroom doors. Everybody in the house except for Gloria had been killed.

It was not until twenty-four years later that Nella and I finally went to the police to find out what happened to our mother and uncle. That morning, our father had driven to the house after Gloria called him, and upon seeing the yellow police tape marking the scene of a crime, he did not stop to ask what had happened. Instead, he drove to the office of his attorney, Nathan Diamond, in downtown Miami. Which the police immediately found suspicious. Even so, they did nothing about it.

Nella remembers...
As we pulled into the parking lot at our school from the roller skating trip, my brother and I saw police cars near the school drop-off. We could also see Louie, the son of our father's childhood friend Nicolas, standing with the principal and waiting for us. He was tall and slim, with curly brown hair. He wore glasses that were very thick, like bottles. As we stepped out of the bus we asked Louie what he was doing there. Where was our mom? He told us that she was running late at the Winn Dixie supermarket and that he was there to pick us up. We told him that our mother did not want us to leave with anyone but her, and so we would wait for her. As we looked towards our school principal, we could see the sadness in her face as she told us that it was okay to leave with Louie.

I had alarms going off inside my head. I just knew something was wrong.

Louie then took us to a satellite police station that didn't look like your usual police station. This one was in an office building. We sat there for a long time, waiting.

I told my brother I was hungry and to tell the police that I wanted to get something to eat at a store next door. They said sure, so I went to the store and asked to use the phone. Then I called my house.

A man answered the phone, and I could hear a lot of male voices in the background. So I said, "May I speak to my mother?" He said, "Who's your mother?" When I told him, he hung up. So I called again and said, "Where's my mother?" I felt our house had been robbed, and I wanted to know what was happening. He replied that my mother was out, and that she would be "back tomorrow". Then he hung up the phone again.

I went back to my brother and whispered: "We're being robbed again! They broke into our home again. We're being robbed right now. I heard men's voices, and I know that we are being robbed." So in my little eleven-year-old mind, that's what I thought was happening. We had been robbed before, and this is what it sounded like to me.

Alain remembers...
Louie then drove us from the police station to his father Nicolas's house, which was about ten minutes from ours.

Nicolas was a childhood friend of my father and at the time was about fifty years old. Nicolas and my father grew up in the same town in Colombia, in Amaga. Nicolas had recently moved down from New York and was doing business with my father. I liked Nicolas and his wife, Blanca, and their two sons, Johnny and Louie. But on this day, June 9, 1982, I felt uncomfortable being there because months earlier my sister and I had witnessed a confrontation between my mother, Nicolas and my father in our kitchen. I'll never forget Nicolas telling my mother that if it weren't for my father's presence he would hit her. My mother responded by saying go ahead and try it, that she would kill him if he did. To this day I don't know what that confrontation was all about, but I was shocked that my father hadn't defended my mother and just stood there allowing his old friend to make that threat.

On arriving at Nicolas's house, I saw my cousin, Juan, my mother's nephew. I hadn't seen Juan in months because of a dispute he had with my mother as well. Juan was eight years older than me and had been living with us for the past three years. My mother had brought Juan to the US in 1978 to start helping around the house. He was about five feet ten inches and weighed 175 pounds. He and I were very close. He was a masculine kid and loved the girls. It was Juan who introduced me to weight training, and to the martial arts—in particular, Taekwondo—as well as to boxing, not to mention rock n' roll music.

I remember asking my mother to buy me my first record, which was by Ted Nugent, and listening to Wango Tango and Cat Scratch Fever, which were hits back in the early 1980s. I'm grateful to Juan for introducing me to all of these things. Today I still practice martial arts, but when I think back on those days with him, I marvel at the violence. Juan and I would be fighting all the time. We would hit each other hard, throwing body shots. I was just eleven and he was nineteen, so I was taking some heavy blows until one of us ran, usually me.

I remember when I was ten years old I got into a pissing match with five kids across the canal. I was talking to a girl that was on the other side of the canal, and those kids didn't want me talking to her. So I told them to go screw themselves.

I had my best friends with me, Lewis King and Scott. Lewis and Scott were my classmates since the third grade at Perrine Baptist Academy Private School. Scott was a white kid with blond hair. Lewis was a Black kid from a lower income neighborhood. I remember going to visit him once at his home and remembered how familiar it was, and how recently my own family had lived on welfare back in Brooklyn.

So while we were arguing with these guys across the canal, my sister came out. I was telling them to jump in the canal, and then to swim across so we could fight. They were telling us to jump into the canal and do the same. One of them called my sister ugly. That raised the stakes. He had said something disrespectful to my sister, so we really got into it. I took my insults up a notch. They finally had heard enough and jumped into the canal and started to make their way across.

My friends and I ran into my house, and I went into my father's room to get a gun, his .357 Magnum. Scott went into the kitchen to get a knife. And Lewis King went into my bedroom and came out with a baseball bat. Nicolas, who was at our house at the time, stopped us at the door. "What the hell is going on here?" he asked. We were all ten years old, and this was insane. So we did not fight those kids with guns and knives and a baseball bat. We did not fight them at all. At least, not yet.

About six months later, I saw one of the kids on the other side of the canal again. We started fighting again, with words. Juan pulled up in his Camaro and I said, "Brother, please, drive me over there. I gotta kick this kid's ass." Juan refused, but I begged him, and he finally agreed to do it and said that he would drive me to the other side of the canal. It took fifteen minutes to get over to the other side. I was finally face to face with this poor kid giving him what I felt at the time he deserved. The dispute was over.

Nella remembers…
Upon arriving at Nicolas's house we were surprised to see our cousin Juan, since we had not seen him since his argument

with our mother a few months earlier. Juan and my brother immediately reunited and went downstairs to practice martial arts with nunchucks. I suppose our cousin Juan was keeping Alain busy, killing time. I can remember Nicolas's wife, Blanca, kept wanting to feed us and I told her that I didn't want to eat. Blanca was a fair skinned woman in her 40's with a slender frame and dark medium length hair. She was nice, caring to us. She liked to cook and tend to her family. I could tell she was a loving mother. I think she wanted us to eat and wouldn't let us watch TV because, I realize now, what had happened at the house was shown on the local news. I said that I wanted to speak to my dad.

When my father finally called, I immediately got on the phone and asked, "Where's Mami?" He said, "I'm here in the hospital with her. She's just very nervous." I replied, "Let me talk to her because I can calm her down. I know how to calm her down. Just put Mami on the phone."

He told me no, because he would be on his way home with her shortly. "You can talk to her when we get home," he said. So we waited. He finally arrived around 8 pm, and when he came up the stairs he was wearing white and blue striped pants. I looked behind him searching for my mother, but there was no sign of her. Then I just saw the look on my father's face. Everything in my body went suddenly on alarm.

My father said, "Alain, Bianella, and Juan, step into the master bedroom." We followed. I sat at the edge of the bed. My cousin Juan was standing behind our father. Alain was sitting beside me on the bed. My father said, "You know, we've been robbed many times in the past. Today some bad men went into the house, and they killed Kiko." Then, in the same breath he followed with, "and they killed Mami."

I was just in shock when I heard that. I felt like he had thrown a bucket of ice cold water all over me.

Everything was just surreal. I looked to my left, at my brother, who had risen, and was pacing and punching the wall, but he didn't cry. He never cried. I was just taking it all in. And then I started screaming. I remember yelling at my father and saying, "I don't believe you. I don't believe you until I see her myself. I think that you've kidnapped us. You just won't leave her. You kidnapped us. And you have her somewhere."

I had only seen him cry once before in his life, which was when his mother died. At that moment, when I said that to him, tears were coming down his face. This meant to me that what he had told us was all true.

Then Blanca came up to me with a glass of water and a pill. She said, "Take this pill, it will calm you." I was so angry. I looked at her and I said, "Absolutely not. There's no pill in the world that can take this pain away." That set the tone of who I am today. Strength was born in that moment.

My next memory is of us calling Kiko's family back in Colombia to give them the horrible news. It was Juan and not my father who called. I watched as Alain stood next to Juan as he was telling them about the murders, but still, no tears came from my brother's eyes. I sat and watched his demeanor and couldn't understand his lack of tears. I realize now that my wounded brother was hiding in a safe place, one from which he would emerge thirty-five years later.

On the phone, Juan told our relatives that a tragedy had occurred, that Maruja and Kiko had been killed. We heard a scream and the call dropped, and Juan had to call again. My poor uncle's family, my cousins, were howling in horror at the news, and my heart ached as I watched and listened to the conversation. Staring at them all. Wondering why my brother was not in tears, too.

Later that night, some police detectives came over and asked us some questions. My father was probably a suspect, because if there's a murder of a wife, husbands are high on the suspect list.

Afterward my brother and I went into one of the other bedrooms at Nicholas's house. We were just thinking, "Okay, so what happens to us now?" We were then told that we were going to the house of Yesenia, who was our father's youngest sister.

Back inside the house we caught a glimpse of the local news. We saw the front of our house surrounded by yellow tape and we saw our uncle lying dead in the front yard, covered with a white sheet with his feet sticking out. His feet are what I remembered seeing last, on the drive to school.

As we were making our exit, a car pulled up, and the housekeeper, Gloria, was inside it. She got out of the car, and she grabbed us. And she said, "Oh my God. Your mother, your mother, her screams... she screamed."

I imagined my mother screaming and I realized this nightmare was all true.

Then, I remember arriving at Yesenia's house and seeing our cousins and Aunt Lucero all together. I just remember wanting to be in my home, in my own bed and not here. Our mom was not close to Yesenia, who was cold to our mother. So when our mother died, the last place I wanted to be was with the people that were not close to my mom. Our mom was very warm and affectionate. She would hug us, and she was very affectionate with us. Our mom and our aunts were not very close, and I didn't feel comfortable with them. I found them to be cold and narrow minded.

Aunt Yesenia was the youngest of six in my father's family. She was a heavy-set woman with light olive skin and dark, straight, silky hair. She hardly ever looked happy, usually with a frown on her face. Very opinionated and judgmental and her tone was always harsh and angry. But she loved Alain. She would smile and hug him. Always raving about his looks–so handsome–the son of her much-adored oldest brother. She herself had four kids, three boys and a girl. I love all my cousins and out of respect for them I'll just say that my aunt was a narrow minded, uneducated woman whom I did not trust. And I didn't want to be in her house.

Our mother died on Wednesday, June 9, 1982, at 9 AM, and on Thursday we were taken from my aunt's home, back to ours by our father to pick out the clothes for the viewing of my mother's body. As we walked into that house, the smell of death was everywhere. There was blood on the walls and floor in our foyer. This is where our Uncle Kiko had been standing when the two murderers walked in. We could follow the blood trail as it led to the garage where we could see the garage door with the five bullet holes in it. As I opened the door, I could see my uncle's bloody handprint on the garage push-button.

We were then taken by our father to the entrance of the master bedroom where Alain remembers our father asking, "Are you sure you want to go inside?" When he opened the door, I could see the outline of our mom's body laid out in the position of her death, with her blood still visible on the light blue carpet. There were two large circular blood stains where she had lain dead the day before. It was so lifeless inside our home, where just a couple of nights earlier we had been laughing with our mother and uncle, just acting as any eleven-year-old kid would act as the school year was coming to an end and summer was in the air.

So I picked out my mother's clothes. It was the same outfit we had given her for her thirty-ninth birthday on February 4, 1982: an ivory skirt suit with a lilac blouse. Then I walked to my room and saw my stuffed animals torn apart and my dollhouse thrown on the floor. With every step I took I felt sick and years later asked, "How could my father take my brother and I to a house where my mother and uncle had just been murdered, with blood stains still visible everywhere—on the floors, walls and doors?"

On Friday, June 11, the funeral home suggested to my father that they should have a closed casket for our mother's service. Our father decided to turn this decision over to us, two eleven-year-olds. My brother and I walked into the room where both caskets lay next to each other. Our father opened Kiko's casket, showing us his massacred face and body.

We immediately decided that the children and adults waiting outside should not see our uncle like this. Our mother, on the other hand, looked beautiful, although you could see the bullet entries on the right side of her cheek. I remember Alain was holding me up because my knees buckled when I saw her lifeless body.

Looking at my mother, I could see marks on her hands and on her face, but I was happy just to be holding her hand and just to be with her. Then I got on my knees and prayed, and I felt at peace with her.

On Saturday, June 12, 1982, the day of my mother's funeral, I learned a great lesson. The funeral director said to us, "Okay, you have ten minutes, and then we're going to close the casket." I was thinking, "What has he said?" He just told me I had only ten minutes with my mother. I would not see my mother for the rest of my life. He had no idea how hard and cruel that was to hear.

Eighteen years later I would become a nurse, and share with the nurses a great lesson, one I learned then. So, to this very day, with my patients and with my labor room nursing sisters, I share that we're never going to rush our patients when they are saying goodbye to their loved ones. They can say goodbyes for as long as it takes them to do so. It's very important that they have their closure, and not be rushed.

At that moment, I just held onto every millisecond of those ten minutes, holding my mother's hands and kissing her. I stayed with her until the casket was closed. It felt like a terrible dream, the ride to the cemetery in a limousine escorted by police. As they laid her in the ground, I felt like a black curtain had come down around me. Everything went black, as if to say to me "that little girl has died" too.

I later learned in therapy the little girl had not died. I succeeded in becoming the woman I envisioned but now it was time to go back and rescue this little girl from the dark abyss of my unconscious. I needed to find that girl and comfort her, and unite her with me, which I've done. But that's the day that the little girl in me died for a very long time. And my mother and uncle were gone forever.

1973, Brooklyn, NY: Nella and Alain age three, in their Sunday best, with their mother. Ivette, Alain's wife, loves this picture because you can tell by Nella's unhappy face that Alain got away with something!

1977, Brooklyn NY: Nella with her mother.

Miami, Florida, 1977: Nella and Alain, age 7, with their mother.

1975: A happy day in Brooklyn: their mother, Maruja, is laughing and hugging her twins on their birthday.

1977: Young Alain at lunch in Coral Gables with Luz and Maruja.

Florida, 1978: Little Nella hugs her Uncle Kiko.

Brooklyn, NY, 1975: Studio shot of the twins at age five. Alain still remembers those Buster Brown shoes.

May 1982: Maruja with her Mother's Day flowers in her home in Miami, one month before she is killed.

February 4, 1982: Nella and Alain with their mother on her last birthday. She loved the color lilac, her favorite, and she is in an outfit the twins bought for her, which they had her buried in.

Florida, 1984: school yearbook. Alain has always been into sports and fitness. Here is Alain, age 14, pumping iron.

In that same 1984 yearbook, Alain saw the picture of Ivette, his future wife.

CHAPTER 2: Beginning

Nella remembers...
I'll start this part of my story by going back to this memory of being a child in New York. Our family had two apartments. Alain and I lived in one with our mother in Brooklyn, and my father lived in an apartment in Queens. When you're a kid, you don't know why this is, you only know that's what it is.

We later learned that our father, who had met our mother in a linen factory in Medellin, Colombia, was married to Estela, a woman who was unable to conceive a child. Our mother was the mistress whom he romanced with love letters and secret dates over the years. He was ambitious and obtained a visa to the United States, looking for a better life. I remember him always telling us the story of arriving in New York City with thirteen dollars in his pocket and taking a cab that charged him eight dollars, which left him with five dollars to start a new life in the Big Apple.

He went on to work in a garment district and brought Estela to New York, followed by our mother. Our father, although a hard worker, was also a hard drinker and a very abusive man who assaulted women and children verbally, physically and emotionally. So, because he was married to Estela, our mother lived alone in Brooklyn, and my father would visit her.

I never met Estela. I first learned of her when I was twelve years old after our mother died. I did see a picture of her: she was tall and thin, with fair skin and short hair. My aunts told me that she and my father had dated for a long time and that he had left her at the altar more than once. He would be found in the bar drinking. My father told me the year he died that he had run into her in passing and they exchanged looks. He shared with me his surprise to see her.

As the affair continued, our mother became pregnant with us twins, and Estela decided it was time to leave. After he hit her and broke her arm, she finally did. She left him and took with her his savings of $7,000, which he grieved until the day he died– the lost money, that is, not the vanished wife. If you ask me, the smartest thing Estela did was to leave our father.

I remember one day we went to our father's apartment in Queens with our mother. Our father opened the door, but he wouldn't open it all the way. He had the chain hooked in. Our mother yelled at him to open the door.

When he finally opened the door, I looked to my left and saw a young woman with long dark hair sitting on the sofa. I saw a round coffee table full of red and white Budweiser beer cans. We could hear music on the radio blaring out as well.

I remember seeing my mother being upset as they continued to argue in the bedroom. I then saw my brother walking over to the young woman and sitting on her lap and asking, "Are you my daddy's girlfriend?" I don't remember what she said. I just remember standing in the middle of this scene taking it all in.

Our mother was very upset, and then she just grabbed us by our hands, and we left. We went back to our own apartment in Brooklyn, and I remember my mother smoking a cigarette and shaking. She would cross her legs and shake her foot in anxiety, while she was smoking and crying. And I just remember taking that all in, too, and it fuels my anger and my sadness today to have seen our mother suffering like that.

The next memory I have is seeing our father coming into our Brooklyn apartment as if everything was normal. But it wasn't normal. I remember our mother holding a raw piece of steak to cover the bruise on her eye, because our father had beaten her earlier that day. He was abusive to her and to us as well. I remember him beating my brother for wetting the bed, or many times, for no reason at all. He was a very angry man, our father, and he was very scary to me as a little girl.

My father was born in Amaga, a small town outside of Medellin, Colombia. He had a very limited education, only going to school until the fourth grade. He told us he repeated the fourth grade because the school said that they would be adding a fifth grade the following year. The school did not follow through with their plan, so our father's school education ended the second time he repeated the fourth grade. We also know that he entered into the military, which is mandatory in Colombia. The Colombian Army is big, the third largest in the Americas after the United States, with a long history of fighting against guerrilla groups and drug traffickers.

I remember my father was about five feet seven inches tall with olive skin and straight jet black hair. He had a sturdy build, with broad shoulders. His ancestry was mixed Spanish and indigenous South American. He was a very serious man who didn't smile much.

My mother was slightly shorter than him, with a medium build and very fair-skinned, like honey. Her hair was curly, but you wouldn't know because she would blow dry it into a wave. She always dyed it brown with blonde highlights. She kept it pretty short most of the time. Her ancestry came from a mixture of Spanish and African people, specifically from Cameroon. Our mother had a very different personality from my father's. She laughed a lot and always had a smile on her face when she looked at you. She was kind and caring with the most beautiful honey-colored eyes, just like my brother has.

My twin brother looks a lot like my dad, except Alain is much taller at five feet eleven inches and in much better shape, thanks to his weight training. I'm petite, at five feet one inch, and I have olive skin with black curly hair, which I got from my mother.

When I think about our mother's family, I remember there were six children. Our mom, Maria de Los Angeles, was the youngest. John, the brother closest in age to our mother, was stabbed to death five months before my brother and I were born. Our mother was pregnant with us when she learned the news. John, who was already a father of five children, had been having an affair with a younger woman. The woman's father and brother had found out about it and killed him in February 1970. Violence was always around us, even before we were born.

Our mother was very nurturing and loving. She was very social, and she had friends in the neighborhood. I had my twin brother, who was my main playmate. I played with his soldiers, and his Superman and Batman dolls, and he played teacups with me. I would pretend I was serving him tea, but on one occasion I served him nail polish remover instead, acetone, as I painted my lips with nail polish so the gloss would last longer. I remember Alain drinking the acetone in the teacup, then running into the kitchen screaming. I could see my mother pouring sugar in his mouth as he passed out. Another memory is of us playing with the dead mice in our apartment. Those were some of our fun playtimes in Brooklyn.

School is where I got my name "Bibi". My brother calls me Nella, but my name is Bianella. The nuns and teachers back then could not pronounce my name, so one teacher said, "Can I call you Bibi?" I dared not say no, and so my name became "Bibi".

I also remember walking with my brother to school, which was down the street from where we lived. We attended a Catholic school in Flatbush, Brooklyn. Every day the nuns who taught us would stamp a card with an angel or a devil on it to send it home with us as a reflection on how we had done. My brother on most days would get stamped with a devil and I would get the angel. In those days they would give girls a pink card and boys a green card. So I would get an angel on a pink card and Alain would get a green card with a devil on it which our mother would stick on the refrigerator. I can recall being very happy with my stamp, and very happy to share my pink angel with our mother, but my brother would convince me not to show it to her.

"You can't show her that or she'll ask where's mine?" he said. "And she'll see my devil stamp." So we would bury the little angel and little devil in the snow, and off we went.

Across the street from the apartment was a vacant lot where we used to play. We'd play with caterpillars and try to race them. My brother and I have always been very close as fraternal twins. We could always find a way to make our own fun, sometimes out of thin air.

We needed each other and we had each other's backs since our father was so abusive and hurtful to us, both verbally and physically. He would beat us with his belt, leaving welts on our skin; but the words he said were even more horrific. I remember a couple of times he said he would shoot Alain three times in the head. Those words never leave you. Our father was a very troubled soul.

It was in the mid 1970s that the cocaine drug trade started to really take hold in the United States and the Medellin Cartel began to make its inroads. While we lived in Brooklyn, our parents started trafficking and selling cocaine. Our lives started to change financially, though we did not know why. We just knew that we went from being on "government assistance" to traveling in style to Medellin, Colombia to see our family for the first time in 1975. In a very short period of time my mother bought a home in Colombia for her mother, her sister Nubia and Nubia's daughters. Nubia's husband was a mechanic and died when a car he was working under collapsed on him, and she was left to bring up four daughters all under the age of twelve. My mother helped raise all of them financially and supported her sister Nubia.

The house in Colombia was in an urban section of Medellin called "Simon Bolivar". My mother bought a four-story house where my grandmother lived with Nubia, her daughters, and our aunt Luz's son Jorge, who had Down's Syndrome. The house was big and wrapped around the street corner, and had a lovely rose garden in the front with an iron fence surrounding it.

You'd go up ten steps to the front door, which was metal. Inside, you took three steps down to a living room, which was a formal area where visitors were welcomed with coffee and biscuits. Passing the foyer to the right was the kitchen, dining room and a courtyard patio where there were parrots and macaws that talked a lot.

The kitchen was my favorite place. It was here my Mamaria, my maternal grandmother, would make me fresh raspberry-blackberry smoothies. I now realized we were fed organic whole foods by our grandmother, as once, this led Mamaria to be so angry with my mom for feeding Alain what she said looked like dog food. "How can you feed him food in cans?" she asked. But it was Chef Boyardee! In the dining room we were served on a beautiful linen tablecloth with lovely china and tea sets. Our meals were always five course meals. There was coffee or hot chocolate, arepa with eggs, and fruits.

The money for the house, for everything, came from selling drugs. Our father was given the opportunity to join Fernando, to become his business partner in Miami, and to traffic cocaine from Medellin to Miami. Our father's intent was to leave us in Brooklyn and travel solo to Florida. However, Fernando, who was in his thirties, was in a relationship with my mother's niece Paloma, and insisted my father bring the family to Miami. Our cousin Paloma was a widow in her mid-twenties; her husband had died of a heart attack while playing a soccer game. Paloma had recently started her relationship with Fernando and was living with him in Coral Gables, Florida.

We moved from Brooklyn to Miami in 1977, when I was seven. We moved into an apartment building with an elevator and a community pool. In Brooklyn, we had no elevator or pool, so we were ecstatic with our new Florida residence. It was here we met Fernando, the man in the drug business with our father. I always really liked him because he was very kind to us.

Fernando, I remember, was of medium build with a slight belly. He had fair skin, and a receding hairline with dark brown wavy hair combed to the side. He was kind and smiled a lot at us. He was known to have a temper, yet I never saw this temper in action. Although he was a quiet man, I felt nothing but kindness come from him. He loved Paloma and she adored him.

I'm not sure how he got involved in the drug business, but I do know he was the one who had invited my father to work in Miami. I also remember hearing conversations revealing that my dad once had an affair with Fernando's sister. Fernando did not like my dad much. Later in my twenties, I was at Fernando's house having lunch and he shared how much he loved my mother and how kind she was. He told me he was very unhappy with my father's "behavior" I can still see him sitting at the head of the table telling me this, with much of the emotion of it being contained. In later years I understood better why this was so. It was just too painful.

For me, Fernando's treatment of us was noticeable because it was so different from how our father treated us. My only other exposure to an older man was with my father, who used to beat us. So, for me, it was strange to see another man his age treating us with kindness. He gave me my first book. I was seven years old, and Fernando gave me a pop-up version of Cinderella. I just loved that book.

I remember getting on my knees and opening each page and being so mesmerized with the characters and the story in this book. To this day, my first best friends are my books. I love to read, and books are my comfort. That which I don't know, and where I have yet to go, I'll find through a book. So my first exposure to reading was my father's drug partner giving me that Cinderella book.

It was in Miami that my father became even scarier. I attribute that to the money he was earning, and to the power that he felt. He had the idea that he could keep becoming even bigger and even more powerful by committing crimes. He bought a larger car, a gold 1977 Lincoln Continental with his initials "OOZ" etched on both ends of the car.

We then moved from an apartment to a small house, and then we went to another house with a pool, and then to a bigger house with a pool. Our father was now wearing three-piece suits and we were going to expensive restaurants, things we didn't do back in New York.

There were all these men around him and my father would speak to them like he was the godfather Don Corleone in that film, *The Godfather*, which first screened in 1972. It became his favorite movie. He would watch it over and over again. And would quote from it in Spanish. And he would show the film to us. He thought he was the Godfather.

However, unlike the Godfather of the film, who was kind and generous with his family, our father was not. In those early years, I remember my brother and I would be sleeping. I would always wake up because I could just sense when our father was beating our mother. One time I came out to the living room, and he was on top of her, punching her. When he saw me, he stopped and he got off of my mother.

He came to me and he asked, "Is it her fault or mine?" And I just looked at him and I couldn't speak. I was terrified. But I pointed to him. I remember putting my finger up and pointing at him. "It's you. It's your fault!" And then I walked over to our mother and gave her a hug.

My next memory was of our mother walking into our room with black garbage bags and putting all of our clothes into them, and then putting Alain and me in a car and driving us away. I was so happy. I thought we were finally leaving this house of pain.

We went to another house, and whose house it was I do not know, but I remember being so happy there. I don't even know if it was one day or one week that we stayed in that little house, but I was so happy because our father wasn't there to torment us. The fear he created was not there. My brother and I would play without worrying that we were going to be beaten for whatever our father thought we had done wrong.

I remember getting two slices of bread and putting ketchup in the middle, as I guess that's all we had in the fridge. I remember being happy eating that ketchup sandwich for lunch. And I was happy to see my mother sitting in a rocking chair outside on the porch, and just being with her. I recall sitting on that porch with my mother practicing my Spanish one day, and then all of a sudden, seeing our father's car pull up into the driveway. He was back in our lives, and so was the fear that came with him. He hauled us back to his house, and then things got even worse.

I remember one day being on the school bus with my brother, and my homework had fallen on the floor. The bus driver was still driving, so I just bent down to get it. The bus driver was concerned because I had to scramble under the seat to reach for it. When she got to our bus stop, our mother was there to pick us up. The bus driver told my mom that I had gotten off the seat to pick up my homework papers. I wasn't afraid of our mother learning this. I mean, I dropped my homework, I picked it up, and that seemed like the thing to do. What's wrong with doing that?

The bus stop was right across from our house. So our father could see the bus driver speaking to our mother. When we walked into the house, our father asked her what happened. Before our mother could say anything, I told him what I had done to pick up my fallen homework. Suddenly, he grabbed me by the hair and started beating me up. He just grabbed me and just started hitting me and I peed myself. Then he took me to my bedroom and punched me in the face. And then I woke up in my bed. I figured he had knocked me out. We just never knew what was going to trigger him.

Alain remembers…

Remembering our father's wrath is something that causes me alarm to this day. I recall that in 1977, when we were already living in Miami, our family had gone to the Midway Shopping Mall. I was in Woolworths with my mother looking at some toys, about twenty feet from where she stood. I walked over to my mother to tell her where I would be, but at that moment she was looking through a clothing rack and didn't hear me.

My father and sister were with my cousin Paloma, one of Aunt Nubia's four daughters. She was always very sweet and kind to us. So she and Nella and my father continued into the mall. I didn't realize that my mother had walked away from me to join my father. As they were all walking deeper into the mall, I walked back to the last spot I had left her. She was not there. That's when panic set in and I began to search for them.

I ran into the mall and I could not find my family. I ran into the parking lot where I thought the car would be, but I could not find our car, either. It was a big parking lot, so I decided to go back into the mall, and I ended up at JC

Penny's. I remember a guard in a red coat at the entrance in front of an arcade, and he saw that I was crying. He asked me what was wrong, and I told him that I had lost my mother. So he took me to a booth inside the store, and they asked me for my mother's name. I told them that it was Maria Isabel Gomez. They called her name through a loudspeaker, repeatedly. Finally, I saw my mother coming with my sister to pick me up. I asked my mother if our father was angry that I had become lost, and she said yes, he was upset.

I remember walking up to him to apologize. He was leaning on a trash can, and I said, "Papi, I'm sorry." I couldn't say it had been my mother's fault because she hadn't been paying attention to me. As I said my last word, my father stepped toward me and punched me in the stomach so hard that I fell on my ass and slid backwards six feet. He walked up to me, pointed his finger in my seven-year-old face like a tough guy, and said, "Wait till you get home." I just prayed on the ride home he would forget his last words to me.

He did not forget.

When we got back to our apartment, he began beating me with his belt, and then he picked me up with one hand on my hair and his other hand on my trousers. As my mother and sister watched, he threw me headfirst into the wall, breaking the drywall near the baseboard and making a head-sized hole. He never patched that hole; in fact, he would later use it as a place to hide drug money.

I remember in that same apartment, in the middle of the night, our cousin Paloma, who was in her mid-twenties at the time, came knocking at our apartment with her husband Fernando, my father's business partner, hidden behind her.

That night, I had been sleeping on the sofa bed because my Aunt Luz, who had also come up from Colombia, was sleeping in my bed. Luz was the oldest of six siblings in my mother's family and was in her forties at the time. She was petite with a very soft, high-pitched voice. She had short curly hair. She was a kind and loving mother of two boys, Oscar and Jorge, who had Down's Syndrome.

When my mother went to open the door, Fernando, who had been hiding behind Paloma, pushed Paloma through the door with a revolver in hand, asking for my father. He said, "Where is he? I'm going to kill him!"

I can very clearly see the terror on the faces of my mother, my Aunt Luz, and my sister, who had just run out of the bedroom and was now wrapped around Fernando's leg.

My sister was begging him, "Don't kill my dad!" I was frozen. In her panic, my sister was pleading with Fernando not to shoot our father. I, on the other hand, couldn't move a muscle, as I was watching a nightmare in live action.

My mother screamed to my father, "Don't come out!" He was hiding in his bedroom, while his wife, daughter, and sister-in-law were in the dining area, attempting to save his life by trying to convince Fernando not to kill him. Eventually, my sister's screaming at Fernando snapped him out of his rage, and he and Paloma left the apartment. What was it all about? Well, my father had slept with Fernando's brother's wife, his sister-in-law. Fernando felt betrayed by my father's action and wanted to kill him. Had my father been the one to open the front door that night, many lives would have been changed. And that change would quite likely have been for the better.

Nella remembers...
When we moved from our first house to a bigger house, our father decided to christen it by giving us another beating. He had a domino set, in a wooden box. On this particular weekend he discovered that seven domino pieces were missing. He asked my brother and me where they were. My brother told him that Larry, our cousin, was the last one to play with the dominoes. I liked Larry and his brother Kevin. They were sweet boys and the sons of Aunt Lucero, my father's sister, and her husband Roberto.

Our father, who had been drinking, proceeded to tell us that he was going to beat us as he walked toward his bedroom to get his belt. Alain followed him and continued to beg him not to hit us but, as he realized his efforts were fruitless, he walked over to the kitchen to wait for the inevitable beating. I watched as our father arrived with his belt and began to beat Alain. Our mother attempted to get in to save Alain, but our father warned her to stay away, or he would beat her as well.

As our father was beating Alain with his leather belt, the belt split in two, which earned my brother a second beating for tearing my father's belt. I ran frantically to the garage and hid behind the refrigerator. I waited, praying for my father to calm down and not beat me, too. I prayed in vain as I saw my father enter the garage and reach for a beer. I came out of hiding and tried to tell him that we had nothing to do with the missing dominoes. He responded by beating me so badly that my next memory was my mother pulling my shirt up and counting the bruises. And I remember her counting fourteen bruises all over my back and my chest. I felt so sore from this terrible beating. I was eight years old.

We were living in this same house in 1978 when I went with Aunt Luz and my mother to the Omni Hotel. My father was at home playing tango music, which was one of his few hobbies. Our cousin Juan was also at home, and Alain was two houses down from where we lived, at our neighbor David's house. David was an eight-year-old kid who lived with both his parents and two sisters who were 12 and 14. My brother had met them riding his bike around the block.

Later on we were told by Juan and my father that when Juan had heard the doorbell ring, he looked through the peephole and saw several policemen at the door. He told my father what he saw, and my father said to let them in.

So seven men dressed as Miami Police officers in dark blue uniforms invaded the house. One of them, a Spanish speaking man, proceeded to tell my father that they were not police at all, but that they had come for the diamonds. My father told them that he had no knowledge of any diamonds. Another man grabbed Juan and put him on his knees with a pillowcase over his head and threatened my father; he had to tell them where the diamonds were, or he would blow Juan's brains out.

As the rest of the men searched throughout the house, I arrived home with my mother and Aunt Luz. I could see a red Camaro with no license plate parked out in front. As I jumped out of our car, I ran to open the door of our home, but our mother stopped me and then rang the doorbell. A male voice from within the house said, "Go in through the back." Our mother said, "No. Where's Alain?" The man said that he was not there, but our mother did not believe him. Our father called out from inside and said, "He's not here. He's okay. But come through the back."

So we went around back, with me leading and our mother right behind me. We had a screened swimming pool and patio area in this big house. So, as I went to open the screen door, our mother pulled me back. "Don't go in," she said.

We stood there at the doorway, and inside I saw four men, all dressed in dark blue uniforms. I remember one was tall and thin, and he was the one who spoke to our mother, telling her to come inside. Our father was there, and so was our cousin Juan. Our father was pleading with her to just come inside, but our mother refused. "Where is Alain?" she asked. She was scared.

I suddenly remembered that Alain had gone to David's house, around the corner. So we took off, running to look for him there. We were frantic thinking that Alain might not be there, either. Our mother and I burst into the kitchen at David's home, with my mother picking up the phone in the kitchen to call our father at our house to tell him that Alain was missing. Alain was, in fact, playing with match cars in David's bedroom when he heard the screaming in the kitchen. Alain and David ran in to find my mother telling my father to get Alain out of the house as she thought he was still there. It sounded as if my father was telling her to come back, that the men had just left. My brother walked in asking, "Mami, what's happening" and my mother was relieved to see Alain safe and sound.

So my brother, our mother, our Aunt Luz and I all went back to the house, entering through the back patio. I could see that my father's head was bleeding and that his shirt was unbuttoned and that Juan's eyes were bloodshot. I heard my father say to our mother, "They took everything."

The men in the police uniforms had taken out the drawers from our chests; clothes were spread out on the floor, as well as the jewelry. We had been robbed. I later found out from Alain that my father had told him he had $1,450,000 in cash from drug money in the house. $400,000 was my dad's profit, $450,000 was that of my father's partner Jaime Wilis, and $600,000 was to be shipped back to Colombia.

At the time, I thought we were lucky to have survived the home invasion; however, we still felt unsafe. As our dad grew in power and money, so did our exposure to violence.

After this home invasion my father moved us to a rental home near Coral Way and SW 97th Avenue. I remember it also had a pool, and Alain and I spent a lot of time in it, swimming and just enjoying being in the water.

Payback for his crimes kept coming back at our father. On the night of April 10, 1979, Alain and I were watching TV in the living room when five men arrived at the house to speak to our father. We were later told that these men were there to warn our father of a robbery and that they wanted to be paid off for the tip. My father told Alain years later that he had told the men to leave the house, and that there would be no payoff.

Later that same night, Alain and I were now watching TV in our bedroom. We were watching a Western, The Legend of the Golden Gun, which aired on ABC on April 10, 1979. It stars a young Hal Holbrook and it's about a farm boy who takes revenge against those who murdered his parents. Our mother walked into our room to tell us to turn off the TV before our dad came home, since we had gone past our bedtime.

Shortly after, we saw car lights pull into our driveway. We thought it was our dad coming home and we turned the

TV off. In reality, we later were told by our father that our mother had left to pick up $50,000 at the nearby Sedano's Market, one of a chain of Florida-based supermarkets. The car lights were the five men who had showed up earlier coming back. Our father was already home when the five men returned to finish the home invasion, tying everyone up in the home. Which included my cousin Juan, and a friend of the family, Gabriel.

Gabriel was the brother of one of our mother's close friends, Betty. I'm not sure why Gabriel stayed with us but do remember he lived with us for a short while. I remember Gabriel, who was in his late twenties, being a nice and funny man. He was thin, with olive skin, short hair and a strong jawline. I now believe he was a drug-user. I remember once seeing him sweating profusely in the car and acting strange – he was probably high as a kite. I think he worked with my dad in the drug business.

Our mother, after picking up the $50,000 at Sedanos's supermarket, pulled into the driveway in her gold Trans Am. As she got out, she could see our father being held in a chokehold by one of the men inside the house. Our dad pleaded for her to come inside, which she refused to do. She demanded to have her children taken out of the house. My father asked her again, "Maruja, if you don't come inside they are going to kill me."

Our mother left the $50,000 in the car and stepped inside the house. My brother and I were still awake in our bedroom and heard the voices. Alain quickly told me to turn around and to pretend that we were sleeping. I then saw one of the men in a blue three-piece suit with a cigar in his hand open the door slightly and walk into our bedroom, checking in on us. I remember trying to keep my breathing even and still while my heart pounded loudly in my ears. As he walked out, I could see Juan and Gabriel sitting on the floor out in the hallway with their hands bound behind them.

Minutes later the man walked back into our room and when he opened the door we could see our mother being led into the bathroom where she turns around and spits in the mans face. All this happening as we heard the beating my father was getting in the next bedroom. This man in the three-piece suit walked out again from our room, and our fear gave way to extreme fatigue, and we fell fast asleep.

The following morning we awoke and, as we walked into the living room, we found our parents speaking to each other. Our father had a black eye from the pistol whipping that he took the night before. My father later told Alain that the home invaders took ten kilos of cocaine and $150,000 in cash. He continued to tell Alain that the robbers had been sent by the realtor who rented us the house.

I remember another time when my brother and I walked in on our parents and other members of the family who were counting mounds of cash in the master bedroom. I also remember the laundry room countertops full of white powder, lit by lamps. I asked what the white powder was for, and our mother told us we had a bakery in Medellin and that we made cakes. Our father had several businesses, two gas stations, five video rental stores, and a flower shop. So a bakery was nothing out of the ordinary. Let's make some cakes, why not!

I also remember my mom driving down Old Cutler Road, a scenic ride we took every day to and back from school. Old Cutler Road remains very dear to my heart. It is full of banyan trees that hover over the road and ringed with wealthy homes of different styles, colonial, Spanish and farmhouse. It is a road where you see joggers and cyclists, and between the homes are these wise, old banyan trees. I cannot afford to live in these homes, but they are always beautiful to see.

I was my mother's confidant, and she would share much of her heartache with me while she drove, which took me out of the role of being her little girl into that of a grownup, even though I was very much not a grownup. My mother would tell me never to believe in a man. She said, "Don't believe him when he tells you pretty things so you will sleep with him. When you wake up in the morning you will regret sleeping with him."

At that point, I was only ten years old. I didn't understand what "sleep with him" meant. I was puzzled. How could just sleeping next to a person make them a liar? She continued, telling me that men, in her experience, will tell you what you want to hear to get what they want. I just stayed quiet and listened to her. I knew she was talking about our father.

She would listen to a song that I knew our father had dedicated to her when they were dating. It was called *"Frente a una Copa de vino"* by Luisito Rey, also known as "King Luisito," who was a very popular singer in his homeland of Spain. His songs were hits in America, Mexico and Argentina in the 1960s and 1970s. She sobbed as she drove and sang along:

> *Frente a una copa de vino yo me rio de mi*
> (In front of a glass of wine, I laugh at myself)
> *Me da una pena tan grande.. Que me tengo que reir*
> (It makes me so sad .. I have to laugh)
> *Y al espejo me mire*
> (And I looked in the mirror)
> *Y me he dicho para mí*
> (And I have said to myself)
> *Y me he dicho para mí*
> (And I have said to myself)
> *Con este tipo y sin dinero*
> (With this guy and no money)
> *¿Quién me va a querer a mí?*
> (Who is going to love me?)

I wondered why she hadn't just left him. Why stay with a scary man who was always so angry and quick to beat all of us?

I look back on that night and realize that this was the beginning of the end. I was in my room at the time. My brother was in his room sleeping when I heard our parents arguing. I listened carefully, and I heard my mother say to my father, "Tell me where she is. Tell me where she is. Because even if I find her sitting in a church, I will kill her."

Doris was one of Aunt Nubia's daughters, my mother's niece, and had been one of my favorite cousins growing up. As a little girl, I thought she was the prettiest of them all. Tall and thin, she had fair skin and long, thick hair styled like the actress Farah Fawcett, in a feathered cut. As a child I thought she was cool. She wore makeup and pretty dresses, and she would give in to my wants. For example, my ears were pierced and she gave me a second piercing with ice and a needle. She would take me along to hang out with her boyfriend on a motorcycle, Carlos. As a little girl I loved her very much. She was my Godmother for confirmation.

After Mom and Kiko died, I was not allowed to have contact with my mother's family except with Doris, who was now my stepmother. So I was thrilled to have some part of my mother's family with me. Once living together under one roof with Alain, I was very much attached to her. She was very influential in my teenage years. She herself was young and so we were more like friends. Being young and foolish herself, she did not give good advice about boys and I made stupid decisions based on her advice. As I got older and made my own friends, I realized she was not in line with my values. Lorena, Jean, Lupe, Edith and Irene all were my pillars of light. I thank God for placing them in my life and guiding my path. I will tell you more about them later.

Little did my mother know that Doris, who was now twenty-one, was staying at our father's sister Octavia's house in Medellin—and that she was eight months' pregnant with his child.

I remember my eleven-year-old brain thinking, "Why is my mother saying that she would kill somebody in church, the most sacred place?" I ran to wake up my brother and told him that they were fighting. He said, "Wake me up if he hits her."

At this point, my brother had grown from a little boy to suddenly a pubescent male, and he was the tallest kid in his class. So I kept listening to them fighting until I heard our father's jewelry rattle. When I heard that, I knew he was hitting her because his bracelets would rattle when he made contact with her face.

So I went back to my brother, "He's hitting her! He's hitting her!" Alain jumped out of his bed, threw the blanket across the room, and stormed into the living room where my father was on top of our mother, punching her. Again, I was standing there as my father looked at me while he was beating our mother. Then, my brother ran towards him and kicked him off her, then pushed him. My father fell backwards.

Our father just stared at us, then yelled at our mother and blamed her. "Look what you've done! Now they hate me." Our mother was so distraught, seeing Alain hitting our father. Then my brother said to him, "You're never touching her again. Never touching her again." And he stood in front of our mother. Our mother told our father, "You see, Alain is getting bigger, and you can't do this to me anymore." From that moment, I think my father realized that he was seeing a young man who was not going to let him hurt us anymore.

My father left a scar on our mother's cheek from that night, from the gold and diamond rings on his hands. I later remember seeing that scar on her cheek as she lay in her casket. But that night, I told my mother, again, "Please, pack your stuff and let's leave." She said no, not now, but that she would think about it in the morning. And I said, "You always say that, and you don't ever go. We just have to do it now." So I went into my room, got a suitcase, and I packed my clothes. I grabbed my Bible. We were attending a private school that gave each student a Bible. It was important to me, and I put it in the suitcase.

"Now!" I said. "We have to leave now." And she said no. So we stayed.

As the days passed, the intensity of my father's anger grew. A few days after the incident where Alain confronted my father, Alain and I were hiding in the family room, listening to our parents arguing in my father's office. We heard our father say, "Because of you, the kids don't call me when I'm in Colombia."

It was then that Alain jumped up and walked from the family room, across the kitchen, and barged into his office. "That's not true. Mami always tells us to call you. But we don't want to talk with you." At this moment, my mother sensed the energy shifting and stood behind Alain as my father rose from his chair to confront Alain. He said, *"Entonces que huevon? Me vas a pegar o que."* Meaning, "So what now, punk, you gonna hit me?"

Alain lifted his right arm back, ready to throw a punch at my father when my mother stopped him by catching his arm. Mom said, "You see! This can't continue. Alain is growing up."

Alain said to our father, "I told you already, you're not touching my mom." Our father realized at that moment that my brother was truly a force against him. Alain was becoming braver, as "fear plus action equals courage" was the equation fueling him. That was a victory over our father in itself. Our father backed off. Or so we thought.

One day soon after, I went to see our father, who was sitting at his desk in his office. I sat across from him, as if he were an executive interviewing me for a job. My leg was shaking because I was so nervous, so I put a hand on my leg to stop the shaking. I said to our father, "Can you please divorce my mother?" He looked at me in astonishment, and said no. So I continued, "Why? You don't love us; you don't need us. Why can't you just leave her? Divorce her and let her go."

His response astonished me. "I do not believe in divorce."

I was deflated. There I had summoned the courage to go to him and ask him to leave her, but he would not free us because he did not believe in divorce. Yet he did believe in beating his wife and children.

It was perhaps a couple of weeks before my mother died when I noticed that she had started to change. She had started to get stronger. She picked me up from school, and she said, "Nella, you're never going to believe this, but I finally did it."

"What did you do?" I asked. She answered me in Spanish: "I don't love your father anymore. And today I tried to kill him. We were arguing in our bathroom, and he spit on my face, so I grabbed the gun, and he ran around the house. I ran after him with the .357 magnum that was in his nightstand. And I shot the gun. But, Nicolas, his old friend from Amaga, grabbed my hands just as I pulled the trigger, and the bullet went up into the bedroom ceiling."

Sure enough, when I got home, I saw the bullet hole in the ceiling of the bedroom. My mother went on to tell me that he was still in his underwear running around the house when she fired the gun.

I knew that my father was going to be furious and humiliated because he ran from our mother in his underwear in front of his friend who was visiting that morning.

A couple of days passed and our mother said, "Well, I found an apartment, and we're leaving." She said it was an apartment in Miami Beach. I was excited that finally mom had taken the steps to leave him and live near the beach. We were finally going to be free of him.

Even so, our mother continued in the cocaine business that my father had brought her into. I later learned she was a hothead in business–and ballsy, to say the least. I recall Alain and I being used as mules when we were eight years old to take money back to Medellin. On one occasion, he and I were running through the Miami International Airport. My mom cringed, calling after Alain when she saw a wad of cash peeking out from the bottom of his pant leg: "Don't run! Stay still, Alain!"

She took him into the bathroom to adjust the cash strapped around his legs. We both had stacks of money taped to our legs. I had another stack taped between my legs. I can still remember my legs throbbing and bleeding from how tight the money was taped.

We finally arrived at our big house in Medellin, with the rose garden out front and the talking parrots and macaws on the patio. But I recall laying in bed, waiting anxiously for Mami to cut the tape off me. To get the money off me. It was so painful. When she finally removed it, I could feel the blood rushing through my legs in relief.

As a mother of three myself now, I can't believe she agreed to do that; but then again, she did not learn how to say "No" to our father. The ability to say "No" was something that I most certainly did learn.

Back at home, in Florida, I knew the time was getting close for my mom to leave our dad and start a new life. On one of our drives together I remember seeing a rainbow. She said, "Look at the beautiful colors; God made that rainbow. Don't you forget it! You have to believe in God."

She then said, "Promise me that if something happens to me, you'll take care of Alain. You won't let him get into drugs. Promise me you're going to finish school and become a doctor." I said, "Okay." And then she said something really troubling. "If something happens to me, go to Colombia and live with my sister, Nubia. I want you to promise me these things," she continued, and so I said okay.

Nubia was the closest to Mami. They shared secrets and were kindred spirits. When they were growing up and my mom began her affair with my dad, she would have Nubia cover for her because my grandparents were strict. When she followed him to New York, she shared the news of our births with Nubia and no one else.

Nubia was saved by my mom. Although she was the youngest, it was Mom who went to work so Nubia could stay home and help raise her daughters after her husband had passed away tragically. Nubia also stayed caring for both my grandparents, Mamaria and Papapacho. My mother would support them financially, sending money from the U.S.

My mother was murdered just a few days after seeing the rainbow and the only promise I was able to keep was my faith in God. I did not go to Colombia to live with my aunt. I did not become a doctor. Instead, I became a nurse, and I'm very proud of that.

I also did not keep my brother out of drugs. That is a story to come.

Our mother was very religious: she went to Mass and prayed in church. She believed in God and the Virgin Mary and all the angels and saints, but she would also go to psychics and fortune tellers. And she would take us with her.

Not too long before she died, she went to see a santera named Modesta who read Tarot cards and was a psychic. I remember this fortune teller revealing to our mother that she needed to leave her husband, that she saw somebody watching our house. She told her she could see blood coming out of her head. Our mother was frightened.

So then Modesta offered her a remedy to prevent this death that she had foreseen. Modesta's husband, who was her assistant, had a chicken and some flowers and rubbed both over all three of our bodies, then proceeded to lay the chicken on its side before pulling off the chicken's head. The bird was then put in a brown paper bag. I think the chicken was meant to prevent the tragedy. Our mother was instructed to take it and throw it in the middle of a railroad track and not look back.

Our mother drove across a railroad track on Killian Parkway near Dixie Highway and threw the bag with the chicken in it onto the tracks. We were also instructed not to look back when the bag was left on the railroad track. My curiosity forced me to look back.

That haunted me for a very long time. When our mother died, I thought, "Because I looked back, I broke the promise, I was not supposed to look back." The little girl in me didn't know any better. But there was a part of me that felt like maybe it wouldn't have happened if I had not broken the spell by looking back.

One other omen of her death occurred, but this one came directly from the source. I remember sitting in the living room with our mother and father. He was drinking his whiskey and telling us stories. He said he had bought land in Colombia and that he was building a house. He was very impressed with himself, talking about his horses and cattle on this big ranch he had bought. I asked, "When are we gonna go to see it?"

This was a very pivotal moment in my life, one that I didn't realize at the time. As he looked at Alain and me, he said, "You are going to get to see it. But she will not." And he pointed to my mother. I remember thinking, "Why not? Why is my mom not going to go?" Then the subject was changed. This moment would not return to my consciousness for a long time, when I finally learned the truth about what he meant. And about his deadly plan.

CHAPTER 3: Growing Up Alain

Alain remembers...

After my mother's murder, I remember my sister and I leaving Nicolas's house and staying at our Aunt Yesenia's house. My aunt, who was the youngest of my father's siblings, lived in Miami with her husband Favio and four kids. My aunt Yesenia and her family had moved from New Jersey to Miami a few years earlier. My father now had two of his sisters, Lucero and Yesinia, living in the Miami area. Yesenia's husband worked for my father managing one of the gas stations on Flagler Drive, and Lucero's husband Alberto was managing the other gas station on Coral Way.

I actually adjusted very well there. I liked my four cousins, so I got along with everyone. Nella apparently was having some difficulty adjusting. She did not like Yesenia, and was soon taken out to the home of Aunt Lucero a few blocks away.

I became closer to the oldest of Yesenias's boys, Eddie, who was in the eighth grade in junior high. I remember Eddie showing me his Glades Junior High Yearbook. It was in that yearbook that I spotted the cutest girl I had ever seen. I soon developed a crush on her. Her name was Ivette, and she was in the seventh grade. My sister and I would be starting to attend the sixth grade the following school year at Blue Lakes Elementary. Nella and I had been held back in the first grade when we arrived from Brooklyn, so I was much bigger than my schoolmates.

I asked my cousin Eddie if he knew this cute girl, Ivette, and he said he had her in one of his classes. From then on, every now and then I'd ask how Ivette was doing, and he'd tell me about her.

At the end of that school year, in June 1983, I was competing in field day track events when one of my classmate's sisters, Bridget, came to see her younger sister Janet participate in the events. To my surprise, Bridget, who was also a friend of mine, had shown up with Ivette. Janet and I walked over to say hello. Now, in our Hispanic culture we generally greet each other with a kiss on the cheek. So when Bridget introduced Ivette to me, I politely leaned over and aimed for her right cheek. Accidentally, though, I caught her right on the lips. We both acted as if nothing happened, but I never forgot our first kiss. There will be much more on Ivette later in this story. When I later attended Glades Junior High as a seventh grader, Ivette was a ninth grader, and we slowly began our friendship.

Ten days after our mother and uncle were murdered in our home, I was working at one of my father's gas stations, which I had started to do on weekends since the age of nine. My father had partnered up on these two gas stations with a man named Ignacio Rivas, and his son, Ignacio. Junior was about nineteen years old and managed the Texaco station on Coral Way and 16th with my father, while I worked on

Flagler Road and LeJeune Road with Ignacio Senior. He was a Cuban in his fifties, and he ran the Flagler location. It was my father's idea to have me working at the station with Rivas Senior.

So there I was, nine years old, pumping gas, checking the motor and transmission oils, checking all liquids, cleaning the windshields, plugging tires and cleaning the bathrooms. I got paid $10.25 a day to do what every other employee was doing, and back then the minimum wage was $2.90 an hour, so I was underpaid. Later, I worked at the gas station on Coral Way and my father paid me $25 a day. My mother did not like me working at the gas station, as she thought it was not something that I needed to learn how to do. But our father insisted, and so that's where I was on June 19, 1982, ten days after our mother and Kiko were killed.

I was working there with my cousin Juan and with Louie, Nicolas's son, on the 3-to-11 pm shift. I remember Louie wore these thick Coke-bottle glasses because he was farsighted. We had full service and self-service. The full-service pumps were closer to the office. At 11 pm that night, when my shift was ending, a Mustang pulled into the station with two guys inside it. A kid who looked about fifteen years old got out of the car and went over to a gumball machine by the office. The kid put a quarter into the machine, but it didn't work. Our father knew that the gumball machine didn't work. He had made millions of dollars selling drugs, and he was taking people's quarters for fun.

The kid was annoyed and started tapping the glass sphere of the gumball machine. Louie came out and told him that if he kept hitting the machine he was going to break it and then he would have to pay for it. Even though the machine was already broken.

I was sweeping up the oil that had been dropped on the concrete earlier in the day. We used sand to soak up the oil and then we could sweep it up. I heard Louie and the kid arguing with each other. Then Juan got involved, and the swear words began flying.

As if on cue, our father pulled into the station. He pulled up right next to the Mustang. He was driving his Gold Mercedes convertible 500 SL, and on this night he had the hardtop on it. My father arrived with Rafael, his brother-in-law Fabio's brother, and my sister Nella, to pick me up.

My father arrived as we were in the middle of this dispute. As I was feeling brave, I got involved as well. I was eleven years old and felt very cocky after watching the film Rocky too many times. I could also curse with the best of them. I was screaming "F**k you!" as an 11-year-old kid.

My father yelled at me in Spanish, asking me what was happening. I said that these motherf*****'s were messing with us because of the gumball machine. These guys had driven their Mustang onto the street when they suddenly stopped. The kid emerged from the car, swearing back at us.

At this point our father reached into his car, opened the glove compartment, and retrieved his .357 Magnum. He shot twice towards the teenager. My sister, who was standing by the passenger side door of the Mercedes, was now hopping up and down, scared out of her wits, and shouting "no!" over and over to our father. "Papi, no, no! Don't do this! Don't do this!"

It was Miami in the 1980s and the teenagers in the Mustang also had a gun. They fired three shots back at us. When I heard the shots, I ran back into the gas station. I knew that there was another .357 Magnum in my father's desk drawer. Louie was also running toward the office. Louie, with his thick glasses, didn't see that the glass door to the office was closed, and he hit that door with his forehead just as I was pushing it open.

Nevertheless, Louie somehow beat me to the gun in my father's desk. When he came out of the office, gun in hand, the Mustang had taken off.

I ran to my father's Mercedes, and my sister and I got in the back seat, while Rafael jumped in the front. But we were not going to chase the Mustang. Our father had different plans, as he then drove us to his sister Yesenia's house, which was where Nella and I were staying.

On our way to our aunt's house, Nella told me that our father had some important news to tell me. He had already told her about it, but she couldn't be the one to tell me. My father would tell me later that night. I asked her if it was good news, and was she happy? She said, "Yeah," and shrugged her shoulders. As if she wasn't sure.

We arrived at Yesenia's house, and no sooner had we arrived when Louie called from the gas station. He said that our father had to come back to the station because the police were there. The police had been called because when my father shot towards the Mustang, he had hit a truck driving in the opposite direction down the street, and its occupants had called it in.

So we now had to get into the car and return to the gas station. When we arrived at the gas station I saw a silver Datsun pickup truck with a little cabin in the back of it. I could see a hole in the front windshield, and a hole in the back windshield. There were two people in the pickup truck and the bullet had traveled diagonally through the front window on the driver's side and through the rear and out the camper side window. This bullet traveled right between the driver and passenger. I thought "Shit!" they could have been killed.

We had to complete a police report, and the police officer told our father, in Spanish, that if our father had shot and killed the kid, he would not have been charged, because the kid was on his property, and he was standing his ground. Obviously, the police were told that the Mustang crew had shot first. It is insane to think it would have been legal to shoot and kill a kid over a gumball from our father's broken gumball machine.

My father had been concerned that the police officer would find out the kid wasn't on the gas station lot when our father shot at him. He was on the public road. Also, the gun our father used was his personal gun, not the gas station's gun that I was trying to retrieve when I ran into Louie at the gas station door.

My father later told Louie to take that gun which was registered to the gas station and shoot two bullets from it, to match his account that he shot twice from his gun. He had to turn in that gun to the police, so Louie later went out and fired off two rounds from it.

After meeting with the police, we headed back to Yesenia's house, and it was now well past midnight. When I was sitting on the living room floor with my father, he told me the news that Nella had told me was coming. He said, "I'm with your cousin Doris now. And she had a little girl today in Medellin, your new sister. What do you think about that?" he asked. All I could do was shrug my shoulders. This man was telling me this news ten days after Mami and Kiko were killed. Our father had kept the pregnant Doris hidden at his sister Octavia's house in Medellin.

Our father was having an affair with our mother's niece, Doris, who was twenty-one. It had begun when she was fifteen years old, when my father started to groom her. I can't imagine what was going through her mind as she was getting this type of attention from this older man, who was thirty-eight and also her uncle. She didn't have the common sense to stay away from this drug dealer, not to mention the fact that she was my mother's niece.

We quickly flew to Medellin to visit our new half-sister, Alicia, who was only weeks old, carrying in our hearts the ghost of our mother. Our father had bought that farm he spoke of months prior. He had never told me about the farm but had mentioned it to my mother and Nella when he had been drinking. "I bought a farm. And you're never going to see it," he said to my mother. My mother thought he was joking. He was drunk, and I learned that you should always believe a man when he's drunk, because a drunk doesn't lie. Our father had bought approximately seven hundred acres of land near a town called San Clemente, about four hours outside of Medellin. Doris had friends who lived there, and her friend's mother Fabiola had a farm adjacent to ours. Our father had visited there over a long weekend with Doris, and he really loved the area.

Fabiola had five daughters. The youngest was Lina, who was twelve years old. I would be turning twelve in a couple of weeks. After a few days at our father's new farm, with Doris and our new half-sister, my father took me over to Fabiola's house to meet her daughters. I met Lina, and we quickly hit it off. Lina became my first girlfriend, the girl who taught me how to kiss.

A couple of weeks later, my father went into town. Doris must have been searching through his things and found a stack of letters. Doris walked up to me, furious, and told me, "Look at what I found!" They were letters from Lina to my father—love letters from a twelve-year-old girl to a forty-five-year-old man. I was crushed.

Doris said she was going to confront Lina and marched over to her house, which was close, about one hundred yards away. I stayed back. I was only eleven years old. What the hell was I supposed to say to Lina? Doris was eleven years older than me with a one-month-old child, and she was on her way to confront a twelve-year-old about some love letters the girl wrote to the father of her child. Letters to my father.

I waited for Doris to come back after confronting Lina. When she arrived, I asked what had happened. She told me she had confronted Lina and shown her the letters. Lina looked at the letters, told Doris to hold on, and went back into the house. She returned with a stack of love letters that my father had written to her. Those letters were postmarked Miami, mailed from our home. My father had been writing love letters to Lina for I don't know how long. It was clear our father had also been grooming Lina from childhood.

As an eleven-year-old, I didn't understand what a pedophile was. I didn't know about statutory rape or anything like that. All I knew was that I had seen my father with other women, and that he had no limits. I mean, he was with our mother's niece, my cousin, and had a daughter with her two weeks after our mother was murdered. I knew that there was something very wrong with this, but I just didn't know that this was criminal as well.

When our father came back from town, Doris confronted him with the love letters to Lina. They argued about it, but like everything else when it came to my father, Doris swept it under the rug.

Doris had been with my father since she was fifteen years old. So her judgment of him was conflicted, to say the least. She understood that she had been groomed as well. We don't know if she had any involvement with our mother and Kiko's murders. In fact, sadly, we may never know the answer to that question. At the time, it wasn't even a thought. We just knew that all of a sudden our father had a new family and that our mother was dead.

So that's the information that was swirling in my eleven-year-old head when I left the farm and returned to the United States. Our father was clearly a dangerous man, and I would later find out exactly how dangerous he was. When my life took a turn. Thanks to him.

CHAPTER 4: Growing Up Nella

Nella remembers...
I was living at Aunt Yesenia house after my mother's burial. Her house was a 1970s rancher with three bedrooms and two bathrooms. And my dad had added two additional bedrooms and bathrooms and a pool. I was sleeping at the time in the garage, which had been converted into a bedroom. One night, a week after my mother's burial, I woke up and could see my mother standing in front of me, but she looked like a spirit, as if you could put your hand through her. She looked beautiful. She was wearing what I'd chosen for her to wear in her casket. She was glowing and radiant. I remember closing my eyes and opening them again–and she was still there. I remember even pinching myself and thinking that I was dreaming. Or maybe I was going crazy.

But I could hear her voice in my head, speaking to me. She said, "Don't be afraid." And I replied, "I'm so scared, Mami." She said, "I'm okay. I'm with you." Then I closed my eyes and started praying to God. When I opened my eyes again, she was gone.

I ran into the other room where my brother was sleeping, and I woke him up. "I saw mom!" I exclaimed. "I saw her, and people are going to think I'm crazy, but I saw her and I'm not making this up!" He believed me, and he was so excited to hear my news. I told him that she had told me that she was going to be okay and that she was with us, watching over us.

When I told our father, he stayed quiet. I heard him later discuss my vision with my aunts, and the possibility of taking me to a psychologist to be checked out. However, that move was frowned upon because it was viewed as an admission of mental weakness, and that's something in which my father's family did not believe. So I was never taken to a therapist. I would only see one years later, when it was my choice to go.

After that discussion about sending me to a psychologist, because I had told them I had seen my dead mother, I decided that I would not tell them anything at all about my visits with our mother anymore. I would only tell my brother.

My mother visited me a lot, in different ways. I would just be sitting there watching TV, and I would feel her presence and smell her perfume in the room. She wore perfumes that were warm and woodsy with floral notes, like Clinique's Aromatics Elixir, and Oscar de la Renta. It was as if the room had suddenly received a jolt of electricity, and I would tell her that I knew she was there.

Eventually, my brother saw her too. He said she had come to visit him, and she was dressed all in white. My brother told our father about his visions, and I remember our father was concerned that we were now both seeing our mom. Everybody soon knew about our visions, and they also knew that Alain and I had been her obsession in life. So why wouldn't she come to see us?

After our mother's death, my father went back and forth to Medellin to visit Doris and the baby Alicia. He had a private plane at that time and was always traveling because of the other businesses he had in Medellin. But none of us ever traveled in his plane. Our father, in addition to the plane, two gas stations and the farm, had five movie rental video stores in Colombia, named "Pulsar".

In December of 1982, my father planned to have Ignacio Rivas Junior fly from Miami to Medellin on a commercial flight and pick up Doris and Octavia, my father's sister, then travel back with fake documents into the United States. They were to be traveling as Ignacio Jr.'s wife and mother-in-law.

My half-sister Alicia was six months old at the time and she and Octavia's two young daughters, who were six and seven, would be flying into Boca Raton's private airport on my father's private plane. On this night we were all excited to receive our little half-sister and our two cousins. Doris and my aunt Octavia were also trying to get into the country through the Miami Airport, but were detained upon arriving on a commercial flight, and both were deported back to Colombia days later. I remember being with Alain and driving to Junior's condo in Boca Raton to pick up our little sister and two cousins. Doris and our aunt eventually made another attempt to get back into the United States and were successful this time.

I had been living with my Aunt Lucero and her family. It was a hard adjustment to live with my aunt as she and my aunt Yesenia were not effusive in their welcome of me, and indeed acted as if I was a burden. I loved my little cousins, especially the baby, Jeanette, who was six months old. And the boys, Larry and Kevin, were sweet and adorable. Lucero's husband, Roberto, was a kind man who always showed me kindness and warmth. He was from Mexico, so I enjoyed his home-cooked meals.

The adjustment was tough physically as well when I went to live with Lucero, as she lived humbly. It was a big contrast from how I lived with my mother. They had a small three-bedroom house with a pool and a nice garden where they grew roses and hot peppers. Her husband Roberto would pick jalapenos from the garden and cook. I liked his Mexican cooking.

But living in Lucero's house was different. My aunt worked at Burger King and they lived on a budget. Rationed food, rationed air conditioning and rationed gas. So I went from a big house with all the comforts that you could imagine, to a smaller house where everything was rationed, with no AC–in Miami! I no longer had a private room, and if I was hungry and I wanted another plate of food, Lucero made me feel bad for asking. "You eat too much; you must have a tapeworm inside of you!" she would say.

Both my aunts were very judgmental and opinionated and spoke in harsh tones. My mother was sweet and smiled just to see me, so I felt sad because I had come from a mother who provided me with anything that I wanted, and I missed her so much. And if that wasn't enough, my loneliness grew even more with my brother's absence. He was living with our other aunt, Yesenia.

I would see my brother at school and after, I would walk with him to our Aunt Yesenia's home, and I would spend time with him and my other cousins.

Whenever I didn't get along with one aunt, the other aunt would come and talk to me. "What's going on?" she would ask. "I hear you're giving your aunt some attitude." In that house you were not allowed to express your thoughts–happy, angry, or otherwise. You just had to shut up and do as you were told. I didn't like it.

I also didn't see our father often, but when I did, I asked him if we could come back and live with him, as he and Doris and their baby were living in Kendall, which is about thirty minutes away by car, and is a lower cost but quality version of the best of Florida life. I did not consider why he was living in a less expensive neighborhood at the time, but perhaps it was due to business, or to appearance. He did not want to be the big shot with the new wife and baby so soon after the murder of our mother.

I wanted to live with him. Others might look at it as a strange desire, after the beatings and his cruelty, but he was my father, and I wanted to live with my brother again.

I wanted to be a family, at least what was left of one. He was living his new life with Doris and the baby Alicia and he had left each of us at his sister's homes in the same city. We lived with our aunts for two years during the sixth and seventh grades. My brother started to get into some trouble at the end of grade 7 and our father then sent for us to move back in with him, Doris, Alicia and our new half-sister Maya. I think this was less about him wanting his family to be whole than it was to have me help Doris with the housework and her two little girls.

But I was happy, because I was finally going to be in somewhat of a home with my brother and with my father. And with my cousin Doris, who represented a part of my mom, because she had my mother's blood.

After Mom and Kiko died, I was not allowed to have contact with my mother's family except through Doris, who was now my stepmom. So I was thrilled to have some part of Mom's family with me. Once living together under the same roof as Alain, I was very much attached to her. She was very influential in my teenage years. She herself was young and so we were more like friends or cousins—which indeed we were. I remember Doris sitting down with me and telling me that she was not my mother and she was not going to pretend to be. She was my cousin. That was a big relief for me at the time because I didn't want her to try to fill in for my mother. I wanted her to be just my cousin. At the time, I was thirteen years old, and she was twenty-three, so I didn't even view her as a mother figure to me.

Being young and foolish herself, she did not give good advice about boys and I made stupid decisions in my younger years based on her bad advice. As I got older and made my own friends, I realized she was wrong about a lot.

Even so, I had my own room, which I later shared with my little half-sisters, Alicia and Maya. Those two brought me so much joy because they were so innocent. I started feeling alive again.

Doris was not only my cousin, but also my stepmother and the godmother at my Catholic Confirmation, which happened when I was ten years old. So she was supposed to be like a spiritual mentor to me but, instead, she would tell me many things that I shouldn't have known as a young teenager. She would tell me about her relationship with my father. She told me that when she was fifteen, my father would write her love letters. Since she didn't know what to do with them, she gave them to her mother.

My Aunt Nubia, her mother, told Doris not to pay attention to him, but she knew that he liked her and that he was flirting with her. However, at the age of eighteen, she had a boyfriend named Carlos, with whom she had fallen in love. She was happy with him. But that happiness was short lived as my father was feeling disrespected and was completely certain that he had also been played for a fool.

When Doris turned eighteen years old our father provided her with a bank account for her to spend as she wished. Up to a point. The money in it was not intended to be spent on or with her lover. In Colombian culture at that time, it was very fashionable for a young woman to be with an older man. I'm not sure what she was thinking, but no doubt my father manipulated her mind and her emotions along those cultural lines. It is also easy to understand why she would fall deeply for Carlos, since he was her age and he shared more similarities with her than this forty-two-year-old married man from Miami. Carlos later died on her lap in a Jeep during a shooting. She was shot as well, and barely survived the shooting.

One day in 1984, Doris came into my room crying. I asked her what happened. She said through her tears, "Your father just told me something. He told me that he's the one who killed Carlos." I was probably fourteen years old when I heard this, but the story got worse. My father had explained to Doris that he was angry because he found out that she had a boyfriend, and that she was spending the money that he was giving to her with her boyfriend and making him look like a fool. So he had arranged not only to have Carlos killed, but Doris as well.

Doris, who was nineteen at the time, and Carlos were sitting in their car in front of his mother's house. He was sitting in the driver seat, as they were speaking to a friend standing by her passenger window. Suddenly, she heard what sounded like firecrackers and Carlos told her to put her head down. When it was over, Carlos slumped over to her side of the car and died. Doris, who didn't realize that she had also been shot, stepped out of the car where the man she was talking to asked her if she had been hit. Doris responded, "No, I don't think so" as she looked down and saw a hole in her left wrist and her stomach soaked with blood. The man proceeded to rush her to the hospital.

At the hospital, the surgeons opened her up to do exploratory surgery and discovered a bullet in her stomach. Another had struck her on the wrist, and left keloid scars. Doris survived, but she did'nt know that it was my father who sent those killers until she had two babies at home and living in Miami with him. Now she questioned everything. "Why did he try to kill me, then have two children with me? Why am I here?" I realized that she, too, had suffered his violent wrath.

Upon learning of Carlos's death, I realized for the first time that my father was a murderer. So the next day, when my father was drunk, I went and asked him if he had murdered Carlos and tried to kill Doris. He said, "Yes, it's true. I had him killed. You don't humiliate me. I gave her money. And she used it on another man. You don't do that. It was disrespectful to me. You don't do that."

Having watched *The Godfather*, I understood the cost of being disrespectful to a man like my father. I realized he was scarier than I had previously thought. He, of course, didn't see it that way. He saw it as a matter of preserving his so-called honor.

Throughout the years he started sharing with me more of his "heroic actions" and told me that he had solved problems for people in Colombia. "If something happens, I take care of it and I'm their hero." He told me the story of a girl who got raped and her family went to my father for help, and he took care of it. He had the rapist killed and his body delivered to the front door of the house of his victim. He also killed some people who had stolen cattle from his farm.

I would listen in shock as he would tell me these stories. I knew he was a murderer. I was scared of him, and I felt shame at the same time. I was just a kid. So I just kind of listened and took it in but couldn't do anything about it. So it festered inside me.

Doris confided in me, and she told me her stories. She told me how much she had loved Carlos, whom my father had murdered. And before him, she had fallen for one of her teachers, who was her first love. And she always thought about him. She was not a good influence on me. She was not a friend. She was a selfish woman, who only thought of her own motives, always playing the victim. It was years later I was finally able to see through her. She was the toughest one to forgive in our story. It is easier to forgive a dead person.

So I was exposed to violence, drugs and perversity at a young age. I recall my cousin Juan, whom I loved very much as a child. He was maybe eighteen, and my brother looked up to him. And he lived with us as well for some time, as did my other cousin, Gregorio, my uncle Memo's son.

Gregorio had olive skin, light eyes and curly hair styled in an Afro. I loved him and felt loved by him in a brotherly way. He was always respectful. He had "kind eyes on me," as we would say– which is to say that he treated me kindly. But I was scared when my mother became afraid of him and took us out of Perrine Elementary early one day. I remember her holding my hand as we walked to the Corvette, her car, and she said he was in town and we needed to be with her. I later found out he was not in good standing with my dad and was using drugs. He made poor decisions that led to him being sentenced to prison not long after.

I do remember being in Colombia and sitting in the back of the car overhearing a conversation between him and my mother. He was asking to come to the US to work with our father, and my mother said no. She did not want this to be. But he came anyway, and after he arrived and got involved in drugs, the relationship then had gone bad, very bad, and there was lots of bad blood.

One day at home I remember watching TV, and Juan was sitting behind me. Juan called out to me, and when I looked back, he was masturbating behind me. That was the first time I saw male genitals and I got scared. I remember fleeing to my room. He thought it was funny. I didn't think it was funny.

I bloomed early and started to get my period at age ten. I remember Juan playing around with my brother in our swimming pool, and he said, "Oh, let's throw her in the pool." He did so, and in the process, he took my shirt off. I was so embarrassed. He had exposed me, and while I loved my cousin, I hated that stuff. It was not long after this that Juan was diagnosed with brain cancer. He fought it for fifteen years and died at age thirty-five.

Another sadness was losing our maternal grandmother, Mamaria, in Colombia, which came a few years after our mother was murdered. My Aunt Nubia had not shared the news with her mother, Mamaria about Mami and Kiko being killed. She feared that the news would cause an early death for her mother. This terrible secret caused a rift beyond repair between my Aunt Nubia and Uncle Memo, our mother's oldest brother. Memo was very angry with Nubia, for after all, it was her daughter who had the affair with my father, and in his eyes was partly to blame for his sister's and brother's death. He did not say how, but he clearly thought that our father's betrayal of our mother had something to do with it.

My Aunt Nubia was devastated by her daughter's actions and the loss of her siblings. She made that clear to me on a visit eight years later, to Colombia, that she would write my grandmother letters pretending that they were from our mother. Mamaria kept asking why Alain and I did not come to see her with our mother anymore. My aunt kept lying to my grandmother, telling her different reasons until my uncle said, "No more. She needs to know the truth. We can't continue to lie to her." So, three years after mom died, he told her the truth. And two weeks later, Mamaria died of a broken heart.

My Aunt Nubia and Uncle Memo never spoke again. Many cousins never spoke to each other again. My mother's family, which was once close, was never going to be close again. All because of the choices made between two selfish individuals. Our father and our cousin Doris. I was sad that my family was broken forever. It was just gone. And so I had to move forward.

Alain, it seemed, had moved on. I remember Alain in middle and high school, always charming and very popular. He won many of the awards in physical activity and he was also very social. He was given an open door to freedom from our dad while I, for the simple reason of being a girl, was denied any outside school activities. Alain made many friends, and while some remained true life friends, others were bad influences. Soon, Alain had friends with whom he shared a bond because they came from parents who were also involved in the drug business. Eventually, Alain became involved in it too.

Alain was expelled from high school for bringing a gun to school. I did not know it at the time. And when I found out, I felt I had let my mother down as I had promised not to let

Alain get into drugs. As Alain got deeper into the drug business, he made the choice to leave home. My father didn't want him to leave, so to hurt my brother he told him that if he left, he couldn't come back to visit me and my sisters. That made it worse because Alain did leave home and became more involved in that drug business. Once again I felt his loss.

I remember telling my father that what I wanted for Christmas was for him to allow Alain to come back home. They started talking again but it was more about the drug business and doing business together. I felt terrible. I remember telling Alain this is not what mom wanted. I knew he had already tried drugs, and I hated that. I definitely was not happy about any of it.

My father continued in the drug business, but to a lesser extent. The gas station helped my father launder money. I remember a secret compartment he had at the house underneath a bookshelf he used to hide drug money, as well as other drug pills.

I remember my father saying that some of the pills he was hiding were the new thing, the drug of the future: MDMA, which is known as "ecstasy" when it's in tablet form and as "molly" when it's in crystal form. MDMA would be used to help with Post Traumatic Stress Disorder and autism, but socially, it was used to create enhanced feelings of pleasure. So I am told.

I would just observe. There were no more conversations about drugs during that period of my life. I wasn't yet the person I am today who is able to speak whatever is on my mind. Back then I just observed and stayed quiet. One night the police showed up at the door with their drug dogs. Doris grabbed me and told me to help her take the drugs out of hiding and flush them down the toilet. I remember feeling scared. I watched as she opened the Ziplock bag and flushed the pills down the toilet as the police banged on the door. My heart was pounding loudly in my chest. I was embarrassed, ashamed and disgusted.

When we were kids, the prayers taught to us by our mother were for God to please protect us from the bad guys and the police. On that day, the police were the bad guys, or so I thought. The police found some drug money, and my father tried to claim it was for his business at the gas station. The police finally left with the money and did not arrest my father.

My next encounter with the drug business happened when my brother was already out of the house. I was at the house and my father called me on the landline, as we didn't have cell phones at that time. His voice was very shaky, just as it was when he told me my mother had been murdered. I knew that something was wrong. I find it ironic that he turned to me and not to his wife, my cousin Doris, but he told me, "They just tried to kill me." I asked him where he was, and he said he was at a gas station. I got in the car and took off, driving stick shift. My leg was trembling so badly that I had a hard time driving his 5-speed white Toyota Land Cruiser.

When I got to the gas station, my father was pale and trembling. He told me that some men had been following him and shot at his car. I could see four bullet holes in the burgundy Toyota Cressida. Then they stole what he was carrying: two kilos of cocaine, I would later find out.

He was so shaken that I hugged him, and I said, "It will be okay, let's get you out of here." And I did. So there was always that fear that violence would take him, too. At that point in time, I knew that the life of a drug dealer was illegal, even if we told ourselves that it was "just another business." That's how our father presented it, as "normal life." I feel such shame to this day to have been part of that world, even though I never sold drugs and was never involved with them, except for flushing some drugs down the toilet with Doris.

I've had friends who have lost their families, their businesses and their homes because a family member was addicted to drugs. When you're in that world, you are part of the chain, whether you are the producer, the seller or the buyer. Eventually, drugs destroy people's lives. Nothing good, and I mean absolutely nothing good comes out of the drug trade. I've asked God to forgive our involvement in this drug business.

Despite my upbringing, I loved my father, and I felt sorry for him when I went to pick him up after he had nearly been killed. This was the first time I had seen him vulnerable and scared, sitting in that Toyota Cressida with bullet holes in it.

Then my brother started coming back to the house and talking to my dad, but it was more about their business. Not a father-son relationship at all. My father was very cold towards my brother. That said, my father was not loving at all with any of us. I had lost my mother, my uncle, my brother was gone, and my father did not love us. I was very lonely and very much desired to feel loved.

There was a woman at the school who led a Christian youth group. I remember asking my father if I could go to her church, and he agreed, so I went. I liked going to church and praying.

At this church, we talked about having a relationship with God—a God who can hear you and talk to you. I needed that kind of relationship. And so I remember getting closer to God and praying for a miracle for myself. I asked for true love, for someone who was my best friend, who made me laugh, and who loved me. I also asked for three children and a home. I even said, "He doesn't have to be rich…"

I now see that God was already answering my prayers. It was in 1984, in Hammocks Middle School, where I would meet the two most important people in my life: Tony and Lorena. I was sitting in my eighth grade English class with Mrs. Rudner when Tony walked in as a transfer from another school.

I loved Mrs. Rudner. She was a short, white, blond older lady. She was an excellent teacher. She exposed the class to history and Anne Frank's story and her murder, along with that of six million Jews by the Nazis. I felt a powerful connection to Anne. I learned through Mrs. Rudner's English class that tragedy and compassion have been a part of our human history and that we each can relate to it in some way. It was in this same class that I met my future husband, as well as my soul sister Lorena. It was God leading the way.

I remember when I first saw Tony. "Oh my Tony, love of my life, light of my eyes." I still say this to him! He was a rebel. He had been kicked out of several schools for bad behavior. He walked into Mrs. Rudner's class in the middle of the year wearing a gray suit. His light brown hair was in a GQ hair style. He had fair skin and honey brown eyes. He was very well built with broad shoulders–and he was strong.

He had a strong personality too. He stared at me with an intent look. He now says he just felt like he knew me. There was an instant attraction. Tony is the oldest of three siblings and was born in Long Beach, California. His parents are from Colombia, having immigrated here in search of a better life. They worked hard, his father in carpeting and sales and his mother in retail—not as drug dealers—and they are very faithful Catholics.

Tony lived with his parents and grandmother Sarita, who truly was his guiding light. His father was not very fatherly. He was abusive to Tony and his mother, and also unfaithful, which led Tony to be an angry teenager but with a deep-rooted faith. He was not the best student and was labeled as a troubled kid. But he had a caring and patient teacher who taught him to read in middle school.

But when Tony came into our classroom, he looked at me so intensely that I felt uncomfortable. I even looked behind me to see who he might be looking at. Surely not ugly little me. As you might expect, my self-esteem was non-existent.

Tony sat right behind me and started to write me letters. It really was an instant attraction and we shared as much romance as fourteen-year-olds could. A few weeks later, I broke up with him, as it was all too intense. But we became friends forever. He also developed a brotherhood with Alain and was in our house almost daily, which gave me the opportunity to know him at a deeper level. I was in love, in lust, and I loved everything about him. Especially his integrity. He never tried drugs and he stood up for his values in spite of hanging out in what could be generously described as not the best of circles of friends. He always had a strong love for God and for righteousness.

In that same English class I met my other soulmate, Lorena, who had recently arrived from Argentina with her parents. She was the first person to whom I opened my heart. She was, and remains today, my daily blessing beyond measure. We went on to graduate high school together and followed on with college. She always had great discipline and was very influential in my studies. She became a teacher and I became a nurse, and our lives have been inseparable. I was her maid of honor at her wedding, and she was mine. We shared our pregnancies together and she also shared her family: with the love of her mother and father I learned how to raise a family. Her mom Edith and dad Roberto Vallebona taught me culture, arts, and a great appreciation for incredibly good tasting food. It was Italian-Argentinian, and my goodness, what a delight to my palate.

I remember the years from 1984 to 1986 were especially tough, and I was praying for help because I felt so lonely. One time while I was praying, I was very sad, and I actually didn't want to live anymore. I was done. My brother asked me what was wrong, and I told him that I didn't want to be here anymore. I just wanted to be with my mother. My brother said, "You can't do that. You can't do that!" So I said that I would not, and I never talked about ending my life again. That's not going to happen. But I just knew that I was at a low point where I was very lonely.

Lorena's and my friendship grew, and she was brave enough to ask if she could come over to my house. I was very scared because my house was not a home. I'll never forget her father, Roberto, who later became like my own father, not a violent criminal, but the kind, loving father for whom I longed.

He knocked on our door. My father opened the door. He was not wearing a shirt and he had a piercing through his nipple. Looking back at him was Lorena's father, Roberto, who was from Italy, properly dressed, speaking like the educated man that he was. He introduced himself to my father, and introduced Lorena, and he said that I was also welcome to come to their house, reassuring my father that they had a good family home.

My father's response was, "No, she can't come to your house. But your daughter can come to mine." I remember hiding behind a wall and looking at the whole transaction and being so embarrassed.

So Lorena would come to my house, and she would stay in my room with me. We told each other everything, and we shared laughter and pain. She would laugh with me, and she would cry with me. She was the first friend to whom I opened up.

Since my father would not allow me to go to Lorena's house, we would write letters to each other and put stickers and stamps on them and put them in the mail.

When I finally got my driver's license, I would drive to her house and stay there. Her mother and father were so loving and so good to me. And until the day he died, Lorena's father always called me his "other daughter."

I will be eternally grateful to Edith and Roberto Vallebona for opening their hearts and home to me. They gave me the bread of life. They gave me love, friendship and family. I learned so much from them.

CHAPTER 5: Crime

Alain remembers…

I started to have visions of my mother when I was about twelve years old. My sister told me she thought she saw my mother in her room one night. She was scared, but I was scornful and said, "What is there to be scared of? She's our mother. You should have said something to her." And then it happened to me.

One night, I was sleeping facing the wall, and I felt my blanket fall off me. So when I turned over to pick the blanket up off the floor, I saw my mother in the white nightgown that I had last seen her wearing. The room had two twin beds, and she was sitting on the other twin bed across from me. She was sitting straight up, with her hands between her legs, staring at me.

I immediately turned away from her, to face the wall. I started to pray, rapidly, the "Our Father." I remember thinking, "Ma, if you have anything to say to me just say it and leave because I'm scared." Then I heard her say, "Doris, Doris…" She was telling me to be careful with Doris, her niece, our cousin. I didn't hear it out loud, but I heard it in my head. I couldn't go back to sleep because of how loudly my heart was pounding with this message from my mother.

In 1984, after moving out of my aunt's house and in with our father, Doris, and their daughter, Nella and I felt the house was haunted by our mother. Doris told me that when she was alone in the house, she felt our mother's presence. When she was breastfeeding Alicia, her first born, the bedroom door would begin to shake violently, a visitation that would happen to her often. Maybe our mother was angry that Doris could be with her child, and she could not be with me and Nella.

In the middle of the night, I could hear pacing in the hallway. I heard pacing come into my room, and around my bed.

One late night, it continued as my group of friends, Hebert, Willie, Tico and I were watching a movie in the family room, while everyone else in the house was asleep. Hebert, Tico and Willie attended Hammocks Junior High with me and we hung out on the weekends. They were wild guys but they were nice, too. Then that night, suddenly, we all heard somebody walking, and we thought it was my stepmother, Doris, walking on the carpet down the hall, attempting to cross the foyer into the kitchen. We all heard it.

We could all hear her pacing on the carpet and then head back towards the master bedroom. Twice we heard what we thought was Doris heading for the kitchen. I finally rose and stood at the front of the hallway where I saw a woman standing at the end of the hallway, peeking her head out from my father's bedroom. She was wearing a white nightgown. I thought it was Doris, who probably didn't want to go into the kitchen wearing her nightgown in front of a bunch of teenage boys. My friends decided to leave, thinking that Doris was trying to get into the kitchen and that we were in the way.

The following morning, I told Doris what we heard the night before. And she told me that she wasn't the one who was walking around. We both sensed it was my mother. Doris was also having these experiences, feeling my mother's presence in the house.

The last night she appeared, or rather a presence was felt, was in March 1985; I was fifteen years old. I was invited to a house party, and as my girlfriend at the time was not allowed to go out on dates, my weekends were free for partying with my friends. Miami in the 1980s was violent and there was a lot of fighting on the weekends at clubs, parties and beaches.

The party that night ended up with me in a massive fight with a group of guys. The only one who helped me was Hebert: he threw one punch, and ended up under a car because he lost his footing. I found myself both fighting and trying to get Hebert out from under the car. That's when I got hit on the head with a hammer. I landed in the emergency room and got stitches on my cheek, forehead and scalp.

Now the party, fighting and stitches went very late, well past my curfew, so by the time I got home, my sister, Doris and my father were waiting for me. My father was drunk and standing in the kitchen in a Speedo bathing suit. My father and Doris had been out at a party and my sister Nella had been home alone most of the night.

When I arrived, with my head wrapped in bandages, I had two black eyes, ears bleeding, lips and gums black. I looked and felt like I had been hit by a truck. My sister told me she had been in her bedroom the whole night and heard pacing back and forth into her bedroom from the hallway as if someone was waiting desperately for me to get home. My sister had a terrible feeling that something had happened to me. This was the last night we felt our mother's presence.

That was the end of this friend group. I stopped hanging out with all but Hebert who did try to help me that night. The following morning Hebert, Tico and Willie came to the house to see how I was doing, my father stepped out on the porch. He looked at them and said, "How come none of you look like him, like Alain?" He could see that none of them were hurt. Needless to say, I learned a huge lesson that night. Violence was not going to get me anything but injured. Or maybe dead.

The handful of friends I hung out with were also involved in the drug trade. Hebert and I became very close, especially because we could relate to each other with our similar family experiences. Hebert's mother had also been murdered; she died in Bogota, Colombia, in a kidnapping in which the police were involved. Hebert and his brother, Lucho, were now living in Kendall after their father had gone back to Bogota to work in the emerald business, leaving them behind as teenagers to fend for themselves. Lucho also got involved in the drug trade and eventually connected with my father in the drug business.

It was while living with our father in the house that was haunted that I also became involved with my father's drug trade. He would take me with him on drug runs. Our conversations now became more about the business he was in. I was sixteen at the time, and as months went by, I started to make contacts myself and eventually started to do business with my father. My first kilo of cocaine was provided to me by my father, when I was seventeen.

Coca leaves are a plant native to Colombia and have been used for thousands of years. As a tea, it has been used to combat the effects of cold, hunger, and altitude sickness. Cocaine was first isolated from the leaves in 1860, and in its powdered form, it produces an immediate euphoric experience: one hit can make you addicted. In its powdered form, it is easy to "cut" it with anything, even baking soda. So there is a lot of money to be made from this little white powder, and I wanted to make it.

My father's old protege Ignacio Rivas Jr. had reconnected with my father, who was excited because he thought that Junior had done very well for himself. He was in his twenties, but he was rolling pretty deep in the drug world, and apparently moving a lot of weight in drugs to other states.

My father said he was going to start working with Junior again. And on their first and last deal, Junior sent his father over to our house. My father did not like Ignacio Senior after their experience as business partners in the gas stations that my father had bought from him. He felt Senior had ripped him off in the sale of the gas stations. Even so, it was Senior who came to see our father to pick up the forty-two kilos of cocaine for Junior. I was also excited about doing this deal because, as part of my pay, Junior was going to buy me a new black Corvette. At the time, I had been driving a 1974 blue Monte Carlo, and a Corvette was a big step up.

Senior showed up with a couple of suitcases, and I packed up the forty-two bricks, or forty-two kilos, of cocaine into the suitcases. My father and Senior spoke for about five minutes, and then Senior and Junior disappeared. My father had been ripped off again, this time for forty-two kilos of cocaine.

My father was now in deep trouble. Thirty of the kilos were provided by an old friend, Mariela, who lived in Coral Gables, and he had scored another twelve keys or kilos from some other guy that I didn't know. Mariela was a friend of my mother's. Mariela and her son Anthony would come over to our parties. She was also in the drug business and ended up later doing eighteen years in prison. No one ends up rich in the drug business: you end up broke or dead or in prison. Mariela has completed her prison time and sells real estate in Miami.

I was sixteen at the time, and my father told me to accompany him on the Fourth of July to see Mariela and her suppliers. When I arrived with my father at Mariela's house he handed me his .357 Magnum revolver that he had in the glove compartment. I waited outside for approximately fifteen minutes with my heart in my throat. While he was inside the house, I suddenly heard gunshots going off.

I quickly jumped out of the car, gun in hand. The gun felt so heavy as I walked towards the house. I could see my father inside, sitting on a couch in the living room, with Mariela and two other men talking. I was so scared I could hear my heart pumping in my ears. I thought to myself, "Thank God! It wasn't gunshots that I had heard." It was firecrackers blasting on this Fourth of July. Everything was OK, so I came back to the car, relieved. I had only ever shot a gun once or twice at the time and that was when I was eight years old at the firing range in Colombia.

My father eventually returned. He had bought some time, but to no avail. The forty-two keys were never paid and Ignacio Rivas Junior and Senior had vanished.

Junior did resurface sometime later while I was working at the gas station. He called to tell me that his ex-wife, Linda, whom I did know, was talking to the Feds, and that my father "should be careful." Junior was going through a divorce, and his ex-wife had started talking to the police to save her own skin. It worked, and Senior and Junior ended up doing a couple of years in federal prison.

I was still in high school, but I had quit in the tenth grade for about a month in March. I thought I wanted to drop out, but once I had dropped out, I wanted to go back. I spent that month at loose ends and decided that I had to go back to school. I told my father that he needed to come with me to the principal's office and try to get me back in. He couldn't refuse because I wanted to go back to school, so we went in to see the assistant principal, Ms. Fernandez. My father told her I wanted to come back to school. So she couldn't kick me out because I wanted back in. I had not been expelled; I had left, and it was time to come back.

Indeed, I told her that I very much wanted to come back after my month in the wilderness. Ms. Fernandez was strict and she was tough, and I had not caused a lot of trouble at school. She thought about it and then said she would put me on an indoor suspension for three days, and then I could return. I figured out that if I did well for the remainder of the school year, then I would be able to pass most of my classes and I could make up for what I missed in summer school. I would get by. And they let me back in.

So I was back at school and I was glad. I think there's good energy and there's bad energy out there, and both can determine your life. Well, some majorly bad energy was heading my way, and it would change everything.

There was this kid at school named Chris who kept asking about guns. He asked me if I would sell him one. I told him that I didn't have one, but he was persistent. My friend Marco did have a gun that he wanted to get rid of, a .25 caliber handgun. I told Chris to ask Tony, Tony would hand it to him.

I asked Tony to sell Chris the gun, and Tony asked me the night before to bring the gun to school the following morning.

The next morning, I put the gun in my pocket and brought it to school. I had two weeks left before the end of the school year, and before I went to my first period class, I needed to use the bathroom. Tony spotted me and followed me in. He asked for the gun before class began.

As I was taking the gun out of my pocket and handing it over, Coach Almeada, the weight training coach walked in and immediately saw the gun in my hand.

Very calmly, he asked me to give it to him, and then to follow him to the principal's office. Tony was panicking because of what just happened, so he started to pull fire alarms. That was not going to change anything, as the coach already had the gun.

So the fire alarms were sounding as the principal came into the office to see the gun Coach Almeada had caught me with. She picked up the gun asking to hold it, and the assistant principal told her that he had not checked it for bullets. She quickly placed it back on the desk, and left the office. The assistant principal checked it for bullets confirming it was empty. The assistant principal looked at me and said, "If there had been just one bullet in this gun, you would be going to jail."

I did not go to jail, but they called the police, who came and wrote up a report, and I landed in juvenile court. There was a hearing, and they gave me fifteen hours of community service. And I was expelled from high school. Just days before the end of the school year, so I wasn't able to finish. I never graduated high school. I completed my GED years later.

The drug life in Miami continued. Shortly after Lucho, my friend Hebert's older brother, and my father began doing drug business together, Lucho got arrested in California with a couple of kilos of cocaine. Still, my father then continued to work with Luchos father Alberto, who was still living in Colombia. My father and I eventually took a trip to Bogota and stayed at Alberto's home for a few days. This was a business trip to discuss trafficking drugs into the US, but I learned some other things on the trip as well.

My father told me why he had ordered the hit on Carlos, Doris's boyfriend: he had gotten word that I was going to be kidnapped while on Christmas break, in December 1980. He told me that they were planning to have my uncle Kiko take me to a playground where kidnappers would grab me. He told me that he called my mother in Miami to ask her if she was making plans to come to Medellin. She said she had already bought the plane tickets to see her Mamaria. In his version of the story, my father said that he told her to cancel her trip and that he couldn't tell her why. My mother insisted that he tell her what was going on, and so he revealed what he had been told, which was that Carlos, Doris's boyfriend, had made plans to kidnap me for ransom when she arrived in Medellin. My father then told me that a meeting was set up to kill Carlos. He was eventually killed in front of his mother's house, and Doris, who was also with him, was shot twice as well.

My father went on to tell me how the beef with my cousin Gregorio continued. In 1980, in Los Angeles, my father was staying in an apartment with Gregorio. On this particular day my father had gone downstairs to the mailbox when he was arrested by cops who were waiting there and taken back up to the apartment. Gregorio, waiting inside the apartment, found it suspicious when he heard knocking at the door. As he looked through the peephole, he saw multiple men in the hallway and so he jumped off the balcony, getting away from the police.

When the police finally got into the apartment, they found $400,000 in cash and one kilo of cocaine. My father was then booked in the LA County jail under a false name, and he was bailed out two days later. My father was deported to Colombia under that same false name and then he came back to Miami with his legal passport, under his real name, leaving Gregorio to handle the business in Los Angeles.

My father then explained to me how he sent Gregorio ten kilos of cocaine (approximately $500,000 worth) and that Gregorio had stolen all of the product. My father then put out a contract on Gregorio's life.

Gregorio, after stealing my father's cocaine with his girlfriend and for reasons not known, stabbed and killed his girlfriend in LA and escaped back to Medellin. The hired hitman that my father sent found Gregorio sitting with a friend at a restaurant in Medellin. Gregorio got up to go to the bathroom, and as he stepped out of the bathroom adjusting his belt, the hitman who was lying in wait shot him in the face. The bullet entered Gregorio's left eye and exited by his neck. Gregorio fell to the floor and acted as if he were dead, while the hitman stepped up and shot him again, hitting him on the top of his head. The hitman escaped on a motorcycle, and Gregorio was then taken by his friend to the hospital. Surviving the first attempt on his life.

My father told me that when the hitman found out Gregorio was alive, he went back to try and finish the job. Gregorio was driving with his little brother and a friend when they pulled up to a stop sign. The hitman walked up and fired at Gregorio, hitting him in the shoulder, then fired a second shot and hit his friend in the leg, leaving my little cousin traumatized.

The third time the hitman tried to kill him, a couple of months later, Gregorio was driving near his father Memo's house in Colombia and the hitman chased after him, shooting the driver's side door of my uncle's car. Gregorio escaped again. Like a cat with nine lives.

The fourth and the last attempt happened when Gregorio was standing in front of his father's house again, having a conversation with his brother and their neighbor. Now, after having had three attempts made on his life, you would think he might be on the lookout for the next assassin, and he was. Gregorio saw two men walking on the sidewalk across the street. Although he was in conversation with his brother and the neighbor, he was keeping an eye on the two men who had now crossed the street and were walking towards him on the sidewalk. Gregorio pulled his gun from his waistband, but by this time the two men had now passed behind him and had started to discharge their weapons.

Gregorio fell and began to crawl up the steps to the house as the shooter fired once, twice, five times, hitting Gregorio in the back. Gregorio kept going, turning around and dragging himself up the stairs. The shooter then shot Gregorio's brother, hitting him in the hip, and he continued to empty five more rounds, hitting Gregorio in the stomach. Gregorio had now been hit ten times. The two men escaped on foot and into a car waiting for them at the end of the street.

My other cousins took Gregorio and his brother to the hospital. Gregorio miraculously survived this fourth attempt to kill him, and he was bedridden for a year. Gregorio eventually made it back to the United States to complete his American Dream, and to make his fortune. In 1984, he was arrested under a false name, Jaime Montoya, for possession of less than ten kilos of cocaine, and a machine gun. The feds sentenced him to fifteen years in federal prison and the State of California gave him a life sentence for the murder of his girlfriend.

This trip with my father to Bogota filled me in on a lot of the family drama, besides the beef with Gregorio. He even talked about who he thought were the murderers of our mother and uncle in 1982. He told me he thought it was Fernando "The Monk" and his sister Emma "The Nun" who killed my mother and my uncle. He said Fernando had gone to the house with Emma's boyfriend and killed my mother and Kiko personally. He said my mother had called him at the gas station and said that they were on their way.

I was shocked to hear everything my father confessed to me and thought about it for years. But it wasn't until years later that I came to the conclusion that the planned kidnapping of me was most probably completely fabricated by my father in order to kill Carlos and get rid of his competition with Doris.

Back in Florida, I was starting to hang out with my friend Marco. I started riding shotgun with him. Marco took me with him on his deals, many times just to accompany him to drop off a couple of bricks. This was just plain stupid on my part.

It was while I was hanging with Marco that I landed my first client "Jay," an Italian kid from my high school who had dropped out. I was selling him a couple of kilos a week. I was small time, but I was only just getting started and had ambition to grow bigger. To do that, I was spending all my money going out with Marco to party at clubs in Miami. We were all underage, but when you moved in that high-octane drug circle, the bouncers would get to know you and let you into the clubs where there were more drug dealers inside. Miami was on fire in the 1980s and I was having a great time, meeting people and setting up deals.

Jay would buy drugs from me that he would sell off in ounces. Jay would usually buy with cash, or at least leave me a large deposit and pay me the difference the following day. Jay would cut down the purity of his product for additional profit.

Eventually, Jay cut the cocaine up so much that he pissed off some clients. On December 17, 1988, he called me and told me that he needed a kilo and asked if Marco and I could provide it. We did, and as I was coming back from that delivery with Marco, I received another phone call from Jay. He told me that he had just received a call from an old client who had five kilos that he had stolen and wanted Jay to help him get rid of it. He then asked if I could help move the drugs at a discounted price.

I told him that I could, but I, being greedy, also told him that he had to keep the kilo that I had just provided to him. He hadn't paid me the deposit yet and promised to give me the money the following day. I knew that he had the money and that he was good for it.

Marco and I drove over to see Jay again. We talked about the stolen product, and then he showed us a red Corvette that he had just bought. We were looking at his new

Corvette when the guy called Jay about the stolen kilos and said he was on his way. Marco and I left.

The next day we called Jay to hear how the deal went down, and we called repeatedly, but got no answer. We beeped him on his pager, but he did not respond. I was driving around with Marco, and my other friends Ray and Alvin, who were guys from our high school. Alvin got a ping on his beeper, and we pulled over to a market where there was a public phone. Alvin got off to make his call, then came rushing back to the car. He said, "You guys remember Cindy from high school?" I did remember her. "She just told me that Jay was killed last night."

Marco and I couldn't believe it and were in utter shock to hear the news that Jay had been killed. Marco wanted me to call Jay's house to confirm if this was true.

I finally called, and Jay's uncle picked up the phone. I knew his uncle, as he used to be an assistant coach at our high school. I asked him if Jay was there, and he said he was not, and asked me who I was. I told him who I was and that I had been with Jay at his apartment the night before, checking out his Corvette. He said, "I'm sorry to tell you this, but Jay is dead." I said, "Are you sure?" And he responded, "I just identified him at the morgue."

Apparently, the guy who had called Jay with the story of the stolen kilos was lying. He was trying to lure him out because he or they were angry that Jay had been selling them cocaine that had been cut down too much. Jay drove in his red Corvette to a parking lot near a church on Sunset Drive; the killer he was with shot him eight times sitting in his car. I couldn't believe it. It could've been me. Jay was just eighteen years old.

A couple of weeks later, homicide detectives showed up to Marco's house because of the calls we had made to Jay's phone and pager. I was there, and as Marco was in the shower, I opened the door on two Miami-Dade homicide detectives. They wanted to talk to Marco about Jay.

We sat in the living room and even though they wanted to speak to Marco, I sat there, too, like an idiot, so they asked us both how we knew Jay. Then they invited us to come down to the police station to answer some more questions.

We went to the police station, and they split us up, putting us in separate rooms for questioning. They asked me if I knew that Jay was selling drugs. I could not say no because everybody knew that he was selling drugs. They asked how I knew, and I told them that I used to buy drugs from him for myself. Just a couple grams every now and then for my own use at a party.

I was lying, but I couldn't tell the cops that I was the guy supplying Jay with the drugs he was selling. I didn't use drugs. I had tried them previously but didn't like them. They asked if I knew who could have done this killing. I told them that Jay had told me about this one guy who had robbed him of some dope.

The other police officer who was interrogating Marco in the other room came over and asked this detective what I had said. He proceeded to tell him my statement.

The detective then added, "Listen, I want you to know that we're not narcotics, we're homicide. We don't care if you sell drugs. But your friend in the other room says that you sold Jay a kilo of cocaine. For $12,500, which you bought for $11,500. You were going to make a thousand bucks." I then realized that Marco had told them everything.

There was only one response I could make, and I said, "That's a lie. That's not true." So the cops took my fingerprints, because they had asked if I had touched Jay's Corvette and they needed, by process of elimination, to rule me out as a suspect. I was now thinking that I was about to be arrested for Jay's murder.

I later saw Marco in the hallway at the station. We both got our fingerprints taken and we were released. I told Marco that I couldn't believe he told the cops the freaking truth. We had our story straight before we went into the interview room that we were not going to tell the cops that we were selling drugs to Jay. And Marco had done that very thing.

Homicide had told us that they found a kilo of cocaine in Jay's mom's apartment. Our fingerprints were all over that brick of cocaine. We weren't wearing gloves. However, the homicide detectives were true to their word and the narcotics guys never came after us.

Marco was apologetic to me, but he had shown his weakness. I would never have done what he did. In the back of my mind, I believe that I knew that I would eventually go to prison. I knew that prison was going to be part of my journey. But I kept going. What a moron I was. My God, if only I had had a mentor to steer me in the right direction. But I did not.

And I had no moral qualms about what I was doing because my father had told me ever since I was a little kid that you could not make a dollar legally in this country. This was the world view of a man who only made it to the fourth grade. It was only crime that paid, and if it paid, then was it a crime?

I was thinking to myself, "Okay, well, drugs are my only option." The 1980s were full of cocaine, especially in Miami. It was everywhere, and I ran around in those circles and my father was a drug dealer. My sister Nella did not run in those circles or use drugs.

When I was nineteen years old I was selling one kilo of cocaine to a guy I knew, John Fitzgerald Rodriguez. It was September 26, 1989, and it was my half-sister Maya's birthday, the second child of Doris and my father. She was going to be six years old, and the house would be full of kids celebrating her birthday.

The woman who provided the kilo to my father that was for me was also there with her young daughter celebrating at our house that day. John Fitzgerald Rodriguez contacted me wanting to buy a kilo of coke. Unbeknownst to me, he had been arrested and was now a police informant. So he came over to the house to see this kilo that my father's contacts had brought to the party.

John saw the kilo, then he told me that he now needed twenty more. I asked him why he hadn't told me that he needed twenty kilos previously? I told him that I could get him twenty keys, but that he had to pay for this one first so I could go back for more. He left to get the money.

About an hour later, he called me and asked me to bring the kilo of coke to his house, where he would pay me for it, and advance me for five more. He said we could work faster this way, and that I could deliver the twenty kilos in five-kilo packages so that I didn't have to transport twenty kilos all at once. I agreed.

So I left the house and got in my father's new Chevrolet S10 pickup truck. I was checking in the rearview mirror, and I could see that someone was following me. My immediate thought was that I was being robbed. There were two guys with mustaches, wearing shades, following me in a brown Cadillac. Looking like drug dealers.

I floored it as I tried to get away from them. What I didn't realize was that there were another five cars following behind the Caddie. The last vehicle in the convoy was the van that had the cops' narcotic dog, Moose, riding in it. I turned the corner and decided to loop around the block to lose the Cadillac tail.

I drove so fast around this big block that I caught up to the last vehicle in the convoy, the van with the drug dog, now, unaware that I was following them! The van hit the brakes in front of me, and I couldn't get around it. I was thinking, "What's wrong with this guy? Why is he pumping the brakes?" Then I looked in the rearview mirror and I saw a flashing blue light. It was the police who were following me, and my heart sank.

They pulled me over, but since they didn't have a warrant for my arrest, they asked me if they could search the vehicle. I said, "Do I have the right to say 'no'?" They said, "You do." So I said, "F**k no, I don't want you to go inside the car."

The drug dog, whose name I later learned was Moose, walked around the truck and alerted the cops to the fact that there were, in fact, drugs inside it. Despite my having told them they could not search my vehicle, the police ended up entering the truck and pulling the kilo of cocaine out of my father's Chevy S10 pickup. I was arrested and taken back to the house, where my little sister's party was in full swing. The police were going to search the house where there were twenty kids celebrating, along with my father and the supplier of the drugs.

So the narcotics team poured into the house, with me handcuffed in the driveway watching the drama that I had caused. The cop standing next to me said, "Tell me who gave you the cocaine and things will go better."

There was no way I was going to do that, so I kept my mouth shut and they hauled me off to the county jail. This was the same jail I had gone to on a ninth grade field trip as part of the "Scared Straight" program. I had been picked to go on this field trip by one of the teachers in the hopes that this visit to a real jail would help me to straighten up. I remember two of the inmates picking Hebert and me out, telling us we would be in there soon with them. We just had "that look" that they recognized. As it turned out, Hebert would later be arrested at age seventeen for selling a kilo of cocaine to a police officer in a sting operation. He went to prison for sixteen months. Now, at age nineteen, it was going to be my turn.

They charged me with possession, conspiracy and trafficking. The bond was $750,000, or $250,000 per count. The following day, they dropped two charges, leaving the trafficking charge, which carried a fifteen-year sentence.

My attorney was Nathan Diamond. I'd known him since I was ten years old because he was my father's lawyer, and the one he went to see right after he learned his wife, my mother, had been shot, along with Uncle Kiko. Nathan Diamond was famous in Florida. He was about my father's age, tall, very well dressed. He represented a number of drug dealers, including Griselda Blanco, "the Godmother" of Miami's drug empire.

When I met with Nathan Diamond, I was wearing my jet-ski suit because I had been planning to go out on the jet ski. I remember he sat with me and said, "I can't believe you're here in jail, and in your jet ski suit." But he managed to get the bond lowered on the third day from $250,000 to $70,000. I only had to put up ten percent of the bond in cash to get released.

I bonded out but still had work to do. I had a small shipment in Georgia from my supplier that I needed to sort out. I did that very thing, and three months later on December 19, 1989, I was arrested again, this time by the Georgia Bureau of Investigation and the FBI in Georgia. And I knew that I was going to go to prison for some time.

CHAPTER 6: Punishment

Nella remembers...

My brother was arrested twice. The first time was on September 26, 1989, and he was in jail for three days. He got released on bond, but Alain felt the only way to pay the lawyer his fees was to continue in the drug business. He said, "I have to go to Atlanta. I have to pay the lawyer, Nathan Diamond, $38,000 by Monday or he will drop the case." Alain was desperate. I was scared.

A couple of months passed, and it was now December. I had a dream, a very significant dream. My brother and I were at the top of a stairway. Clouds surrounded us. Alain held my hand and said, "Nella, I'm going to have to go away for a little bit, but I'll be back." And I said, "No, where are you going?" He just said again that he had to go, but that he would return. Then I woke up.

I told my brother that I'd had a dream, and that I didn't think he should go to Atlanta. I told him that I had a bad feeling, and that he was not going to come back. He might even go to jail.

He considered what I had said, then replied, "I have to do this. I have to pay this guy and then I'm going to get out." I told him that our mother never wanted him to be involved in drugs, and that I didn't want it either. I even gave him my Christmas present early. I had recorded some music on a tape, and I gave it to him to hear on the road on his way to Atlanta. He was wearing red sweatpants, and I remember watching him walk away. I just knew in my heart that he was not coming back soon.

So on December 19, 1989, he called me from Atlanta to tell me that he had been arrested. And I knew that this was it for him, because that was his second arrest for drugs.

I told my father that he had to leave the country. He could not stay here because the police wanted to arrest my father as well.

I had just graduated from high school and I was in college at the time and working at an ob-gyn office as a file clerk. The practice was Doctors Aden, James, Zellner and Dimino. Most of the doctors were Jewish. Dr. Aden was very witty, and often grouchy, but not with me. He was from Boston and had that Boston accent. He was a good son and would always visit his mom at lunchtime. When she died, he asked me to come over to her place and pick out whatever I could use, which was very kind and generous.

Dr. Zellner was funny and sweet and never judgmental. He was a great doctor and a kind man to work for. Dr. Dimino was also a very kind man to me. I babysat all his kids and in the process got to see all the Disney movies I had never heard of before! I learned different parenting styles from the doctors. It was a period of growth for me, personally and career-wise. I learned in this office how to file, draw blood, and work as a medical assistant and a secretary. I met my future self, who would go on to be a labor and delivery nurse, as well as a wife and mother.

I also met Yoli, a registered nurse from Colombia who worked in labor and delivery at Baptist Hospital. Wow, I thought, a respected Colombian woman who was living my dream. Ten years later we were working together. She worked in the office along with Annabel, another nurse who was also Colombian. They were both my inspirations to keep moving forward on my path.

At the time, everything I was earning was going to buy food and diapers for my new baby sister, Tatiana, who was born a few weeks after Alain's arrest. I was asked to help the household. Our father had made money selling drugs but was not good at managing it, and so it was now all on me.

One morning after Alain's arrest in Georgia, my father called me at work and told me that he was hearing voices outside. People were banging on the door trying to get into his house. He didn't know who. I didn't know where his wife was, but he was holding the baby. So I was nineteen years old at the time, and I left work and went to his house. And when I arrived, I saw a tow truck and some men. They said that they were there to repossess the car, and I realized that my father had not made his car payments.

That car was my father's most prized possession. Its loss was going to hurt. The first time he ever made money he bought himself a car, and so his cars became a kind of totem of his success. I went into the house, and I told my father that the men were here to repossess the car, and that I would get everything out of it for him. The look on his face was as if someone he loved had died. Despite all of the pain he had inflicted upon me, I could still feel his pain, and I felt sad for my father. So I went back to the car and took out everything. I saw that the repo guys had made a hole in the garage door when they were trying to break in to take the car. It was embarrassing. Especially now, with the neighbors watching.

After the car was towed, I sat with my father and told him that he had to go to Colombia. He had a farm there, he had land, and he had to think of it as his retirement, because if he stayed here he was going to wind up in jail, along with Alain. As a result, Doris and my three little sisters left for Colombia. My little sisters and I were close, and they didn't want to go. They wanted to stay in Miami with me, but I did not have the means to make that happen.

My father thought that I was going to go with him to Colombia. I told him that I was not, and he said that if I stayed in the U.S., then he could not help me. I told him that I would figure it out.

Later, I drove my father to the airport. He was drunk. I know it was hard for him to leave everything behind; But he had to leave. When he was gone, I went back to the house and sat in bed thinking: my mother was dead, my father was in Colombia, and my brother was in prison. I was completely alone.

About two months later, I came home and found a foreclosure notice taped to the front door. I didn't even know what foreclosure meant. But there was a lockbox on the door and the notice said, "You may not come onto this property. It is owned by the bank." I was locked out.

My father never prepared me for that. In 1989 and 1990, we were not walking around with cell phones. We used landlines, which I could not use because I could not get into the house. I couldn't contact my brother, who was in prison. I started crying because I felt like I was homeless. I didn't know what I was going to do.

So I pulled myself together and went to a public phone and called my best friend, Lorena. I was crying and she said, "Come to my house. You can live with us." Then I called Tony, who was my brother's best friend and mine at the time, and I was still crying.

He said he would come right over to help me. He did, and he broke a window so that I could get inside the house. So I stayed in the house for a few more days.

My friendship with Tony only became stronger in 1989, when I was on my own. At twenty-one years of age, our attraction grew, and we fell in love, real grown-up love. Tony went on to graduate from college, and his priority was to care for his mother and siblings because his father had left them. Tony then helped his mother with the finances and by caring for the family. He is a loyal friend, a responsible son, brother, husband and father. His family comes first.

Our friendship grew into love and marriage. I have the privilege of growing up with him and sharing our vulnerabilities. He is my greatest love.

At the doctors' office where I worked, I met my two other fairy godmothers who gave me the gift of friendship, hope and love. Edith, Lorena's mom, was my first fairy godmother.

Edith, now 86, is still working as the director of her daycare. She is always caring and helping others. She taught me, "*Bibi voz sabes que nuestra mision es ayudar... que despues cuando nos vemos por ahogar nos viene la salvacion.*" (Bibi, you know our mission is to always help others...later in helplessness we will receive our salvation.)

She is my hero. I want to grow old like her. She taught me to keep fighting, to speak up, to say the truth: she would say, "Best be red in the face for a minute than to live in agony a lifetime". She taught me history, culture, manners, etiquette. She is so proud of me, always boasting of what I have done. I love Edith. Her husband Roberto died a few years back. He was so loving and kind, he wore his heart on his sleeve. He was also tough as nails. He would speak up and fight against injustice. He stood up to my dad and encouraged the friendship between Lore and me. And I was by his side when he took his last breath. I felt his love.

My next fairy godmother is Lupe. She was from Colombia and her husband was Italian-American. She was the medical assistant to Dr. Zellner. She had a heavy New

York accent and was so loving and funny. She loved to hug me, and I was always in need of a hug. As our friendship grew over sharing tea and toast at the office, she invited me to her home. She said, "Bibi, come to my house. I have two girls that would love to meet you."

I immediately bonded with her daughters, Jean and Debbie. Jean was one year older than me and very bold and strong. She was loud and spoke her mind. I loved it! Debbie was younger and very funny. The youngest, John, was in school and kept to himself. Jean quickly learned of my life story and took me in like a sister. I felt so lucky: I had Lorena and Jean. Jean would take me to TJMaxx, and we would look for deals on clothes. We also went to the flea market to the thrift shops, and we often ate dinner together.

When Jean found out about the foreclosure, she took it upon herself to put an ad on a flier that there would be a "moving sale" on the weekend. So, on that weekend Jean was negotiating and selling everything in that house. Light fixtures, stove, you name it, she sold it. After she had done so, she gave me all the cash. And with that money, I paid for two semesters in college. I went to live with Lorena and I also stayed many nights at Lupe's, sharing a bed with Jean.

Lorena's mother Edith was a strong woman, and she told me that nothing in life was free, and that she would not be doing me any favors if she did not teach me that. She said that in exchange for money, she would cook for me and clean this room I lived in, which was mine. I agreed, and onward we went.

So I went to school, and I worked, and I paid Edith $300 a month. My brother was in prison. He would call me collect, and never ever did I deny my brother a collect call. I had to continue to work at three jobs to pay for those collect calls, because they were quite expensive for me at the time.

My schedule was as follows: at 6 am I would head for class at college. From 9 to 5 I would work at the ob-gyn office. On Tuesdays and Thursdays I had two classes from 6-9:30 pm at the college. And on Monday and Tuesday and Wednesday I would work from 6 to 10 pm at the hospital in the medical records department. On the weekends I worked for a babysitting agency and made cash.

In this office, I also met my other fairy godmother, Thelma. She was a very smart woman and the surgical coordinator to the ob-gyn office. She knew that I was studying to someday be a nurse, and I knew that I wanted to be a labor and delivery nurse. She took an interest in me. She had four kids of her own who were grown up. Two were lawyers and two were doctors. I was impressed.

One day, she offered me a book to read as she wanted to know what I thought of it. It was John Grisham's The Firm. After reading it she would interrogate me and we had great discussions. She wanted to talk about it, so we did, and she was the first person who said, "You're pretty smart, my little petunia."

I was surprised, and flattered, and responded "I am?" She said that I was and that she was going to give me another book, this one being Cain and Abel by Jeffrey Archer. I loved it. We talked about it too, and then she would keep giving me books. She opened my mind, and she told me I was smart. She would also invite me over to her house after work at times, or whenever I was free, and we would go for a walk. We walked, talked, and shared opinions. She listened to my opinions and she gave me a feeling of self-worth.

As often as I could, I would drive to Atlanta to visit my brother in prison. I had to be strong for Alain, and Alain would be strong for me. He would smile and we would put up this front. But, I would break down afterwards because it was so hard to see him in an orange jumpsuit and shackled at his ankles and his wrist. He was my brother, my twin brother, and it was painful.

I couldn't believe that somebody had murdered my mother, and they were still out there, and her son was the one who was now in prison.

On the day of Alain's sentencing, I went to court by myself. He was wearing a blue jacket, and he smiled at me. I smiled back, but inside I was a mess of emotions. I was about to lose my twin brother for a long time. The prosecution wanted to give him a thirty-year sentence, and I felt this pain in my stomach at the fact I might not be in the same room, free, with my brother again until we were in our fifties.

Alain's lawyer now was Howard Manchel, who was a nice man and worked hard for Alain. But I was afraid there was not much he could do. As a last resort, a "Hail Mary" kind of play, he decided to put me up on the stand. I was to convince the judge that my brother deserved a reduction under "extraordinary circumstances."

Mr. Manchel knew about those circumstances. He had asked my brother the day before sentencing to tell him about everyone in the family who had been arrested for narcotics. My brother proceeded to tell him about Kiko in 1979, our aunt Luz in 1980, our cousin Juan in 1984, our aunt Yesenia in the 1980s and my cousin Gregorio in 1984. He also spoke of the murders of our mother and Uncle Kiko.

In court the next day, when it was my turn, I went up on the stand. I don't know how I didn't cry, but my leg was shaking very badly as it did when I was afraid, or very nervous, or both. Mr. Manchel was aggressive in proving his point, telling Judge J. Owen Forrester that we were all soldiers of my father. And my brother was refusing to cooperate with the prosecution, not in order to protect our father; he was staying silent to protect me.

I said to Mr. Manchel, "You don't understand. We've already lost our mother and an uncle to murder, and we've experienced home invasions. So the threat from outside forces to us is very real." I added that Alain's supplier had already come to my place of work to demand proof that he was in jail and that he had not just vanished with the merchandise on his last trip to Atlanta. I had to show him documents that he was in prison. So Alain's supplier knew who I was and also where our family was now living in Colombia.

Mr. Manchel wanted me to explain that, despite these traumatic events, how we got to here. I told him that I worked at a doctor's office and was in college, while Alain had become a drug dealer. I said, "Well, maybe because when our mom died, Alain went to live with one aunt, and I went to live with another aunt who worked at Burger King. Everyone else who was connected to our father was affected by his business. Everyone." At that point, I really didn't care what they thought about me, or that I was exposing my aunt and my father. I was trying to save my brother from three decades in prison.

I said, "You know, my father is a drug dealer." Then I looked at Judge Forrester. He was an older white man, older than my father, and had always worked and practiced law in Georgia. And at this point, the influence that I'd had from Thelma kicked in, because the next thing I said to the judge, "You know, I'm sure your son goes to law school, or I'm sure he goes to college, and he's learned a lot from you. But my father was a drug dealer. And so that was what my brother learned. That's what he saw as a way to get out. When my father kicked him out in the streets, instead of him going to college, he just went and did what my father did, and he sold drugs. In our world, it wasn't looked at as you're selling drugs. It was that you were simply running an illegal business. They didn't understand what it really was."

I told him that my brother and I were born here, in the United States, and that it wasn't our fault that our parents were drug dealers. And yet, "Somewhere out there are the people who murdered our mother and uncle, and you're not looking for them. But here you have my mother's son, and you want to put him in prison for thirty years."

I looked at Judge Forrester again, and I said, "I know he needs to be punished, because it was wrong for him to do what he did. I am just asking that you don't punish him for thirty years, if you can, please, so that he can come out young enough to go to school and have a life?"

The judge then listened to Mr. Manchel's closing statements and took a recess to consider Alain's downward spiral. He requested that we reconvene shortly afterward. When Judge Forrester returned, he made the ruling to reduce Alain's sentencing guidelines by 4 points, which were equivalent to 7 years. This brought his sentencing guideline down from 19.5 years to 12.5 years. I realized that what I said had made an impact. Then the judge added restrictions for when Alain would be released, saying that he could not live in the Miami area for five years during his supervised release federal probation, but that this was not punitive. It was to protect him and keep him away from the people who he had surrounded himself with who had led him to where he was now.

My brother was excited, and he was happy. "Nella, you saved me! You did it!" is what he said. For me, it was another loss. My mother was dead, my father had gone back to Colombia, and my brother and I were going to be in our early thirties when I would next see him as a free man.

I was studying and working several jobs at the beginning of Alain's sentence. I was frustrated, I was tired, and I thought that I was never going to finish college until I was eighty years old. I really wanted to be a nurse, and it was going to take forever. I was living with my best friend Lorena, and we were both struggling.

Thelma, the surgical coordinator to the ob-gyn office, had always said to me, "You know, if I ever win the lotto, I'm going to pay for you to go to school. I want you just to go to school, I don't want you doing anything else."

It was 1996 when she called me at another office where I was working. She said that her ex-husband had invested their money and something good had happened with their investments and she didn't have to work anymore. I was happy for her, but there was more. She asked me how much money I earned each year. I told her about $12,000. She said, "Okay, I want you to quit all your jobs. I want you to go to school full-time. I will pay for it."

I was so prideful that I turned her down. I said that this offer was so sweet of her, but that I could not accept it because I wanted to do this for myself. I had promised my mother that I would go to college and have a career, and I wanted to say that I had done it all by myself.

So I went home and spoke with Tony about Thelma's kind offer. He told me that sometimes we all need help, and that it was just fine, indeed, a blessing, when help like this came to us. I struggled with that because I was so committed to making it on my own. Tony said, "I think you should graciously accept her most generous offer."

The next day, I called Thelma, and I said, "Yes please, and thank you." I was able to quit my other jobs, and I registered full-time to go to nursing school. Thanks to her, I was able to finish nursing school and get my Licensed Practical Nurse qualification. As an LPN, I was a healthcare professional and could provide basic care for patients in hospitals, nursing homes, and private homes. And then from there, I made my transition to RN, a Registered Nurse.

I told Thelma that my Hospital offered tuition reimbursement and she no longer needed to pay for my Career. But I was so grateful for her generosity. She gave me that head start I needed. She helped me tremendously because not only did she believe in me, she also gave me the money to go to school full-time with a monthly income of $1,000. So I could relax and go to school.

But Thelma's generosity didn't stop there. Upon graduation she surprised me yet again with a car! Wrapped in red ribbon. I couldn't believe this overwhelming act of kindness. It has been twenty-eight years since that moment, and I value her more and more and will forever be grateful. She changed my life!

So, I have three fairy godmothers. I have Edith, whom I call Nonna, the mother of my best friend, Lorena. She taught me how to be a mother, and a wife, and how to manage a household as well as strengthen my spirituality. And then I have my Thelma, my Jewish godmother. She is the one who taught me about the essential importance of education and how to live a professional life, how to succeed, how to see people differently, and to be open to people from different cultures and religions. She believed in me and was the first person to tell me I was smart! And then I have my other fairy godmother, who is Lupe. She gave me love, comfort and hugs, and also opened her home to me where I gained a lifetime friendship and sisterhood.

These three women gave me love and changed my life. I learned something from each one. They helped me to build my emotional and intellectual resilience.

When they say "it takes a village" that's very true. You know you can lose pretty much everything in your life, but if people step in to help you, then anything can happen. I am living proof of that. I was blessed then, and I'm still blessed to this day.

Thelma and I talk regularly, and she's now almost eighty years old. She has told me that of all the things she did with her money, the one that she was most proud of was me. She saw that I got my nursing degree, then, a decade later, on my own, I got my bachelor's degree. Nobody in my family thought about helping me in school, but this woman, who's not my biological family, did help me. And thanks to her, I've been able to have the family that I have, to be a better provider for them, and to help so many people and patients.

When I was about to get my nursing degree, I remember speaking with my father in Colombia. I told him that I was happy. I would graduate in August, and I already had a job lined up at Baptist Hospital. And so, at the age of twenty-seven, I was a nurse, and I had a diamond wedding ring from Tony, and I was pregnant. And I knew I was pregnant with a daughter. Her name would be Isabella Maria, after my mother. I wanted to prove to my father that a woman could succeed on her terms. Now I had done that. He said that he was very proud of me.

There was a lot of violence going on at that time during the presidential election in Colombia, and I was worried about my father. I told him that he should leave the farm because there had been shootings, and he had already received threats. He said, "I'm not going anywhere. If they want to kill me, then they can kill me right here."

And that's exactly what happened a month to the day later, on June 30, 1998. I had just arrived home from nursing school. My husband was the one who had to give me the news. My father had just dropped off Doris at work. Two motorcycles came up suddenly, and the assassins shot him from each side of the car, striking him multiple times in the head. I couldn't believe it.

I had lost both parents to murder, and here I was pregnant and about to graduate, and I had a very important test to take the next day. So I gathered all my strength and took the test, and I got an A on it. Then I boarded a plane to Colombia to bury my father. With my parents dead, and my brother in prison. I became the rock of the family pretty much. And my mission was to not let anyone down.

CHAPTER 7: The Truth Shall Set You Free

Alain remembers...

Upon my arrest in Atlanta, I was sent to the Atlanta Penitentiary to wait for sentencing. This enormous, worn-down place was just what I expected from what I had seen in the movies like the Escape from Alcatraz.

So I entered the penitentiary, where I spent the next thirteen months. It was in my eleventh month prior to my sentencing when I was sent to solitary confinement for fighting: the SHU, or Special Housing Unit, was also called "The Hole." While I was in solitary, I began to read the Bible. I started to truly reflect on my life and look back at all that had happened and all that I had done with my life to put me where I was.

I had lost my freedom and I was now in a jail within a prison. How low could I get? The Bible, at first, was an outlet for me to kill time in solitary, but as time went on, it began slowly to catch my interest. Even though I had been raised Roman Catholic, I didn't know what it meant to be a Catholic—or a Christian, for that matter. I just knew that Jesus had died two thousand years ago to redeem our sins. What could he do for me now? While I was in the hole I was sentenced to one hundred fifty-one months in federal prison and transferred to complete my sentence in Texarkana, Texas, in a medium security prison.

I had been in Texarkana for six months when the State of Florida warrant division requested my presence back in Florida to face charges for trafficking cocaine. When I arrived in Miami, a public defender was now representing me because I couldn't complete my prior attorney Nathan Diamond's fee. My public defender filed a motion to suppress the evidence and won. He went after the cops, asking why they were chasing me? Was I speeding, and if so where was the ticket? And despite my telling them not to check the truck, they did. My attorney really made the arresting police officer look incompetent on the stand.

The judge agreed that the search of my father's Chevrolet S10 pickup that I was driving was illegal. There was no warrant for my arrest, the stop was illegal, and when I was asked if they could search the truck I had said no. So my attorney literally turned to me and exclaimed, "Motherf***er, you won!"

The problem was that it was not a total victory, as I still had to go back to Texarkana to complete a twelve-year sentence. I said to him, "What now?" He said, "Tomorrow they'll bring me back and drop the charges." "Beautiful!" I replied.

The following day, instead of me going to court to get my charges dropped, my attorney visited me in the Dade County Jail and proceeded to tell me, "Houston, we have a problem. The prosecutor has appealed the judge's decision on the motion to suppress and you now have to wait here for the appellate court to decide." I asked how long that wait would be. He said maybe six months. What? I couldn't believe it. I'd just left Texarkana, where they had two weight piles, tennis courts, a soccer field, basketball and bocce courts: I was at Club Fed. And now here I was sitting in a hell hole in Miami. God only knew what was about to come my way. And I mean that literally.

It was June of 1991, and while waiting in Miami, I started to attend church meetings. I remember one afternoon watching two Black males sitting facing each other, studying the Bible. Then suddenly, I saw one running after the other with a pen, trying to stab him in the back. For the life of me, I couldn't understand what they could have been talking about to get one of them to react that way. The other inmates laughed at them in derision, calling them Jesus freaks.

My thought at the time about Christians was that they were hypocrites for asking for God's help to get them out of trouble, when, if they had been true Christians, they would not have landed in trouble in the first place. I had seen and heard so many times before that people in the drug business pray for shipments of cocaine to arrive so drug traffickers could make money for themselves or pray to keep the police away. Myself included. I prayed whenever there was trouble in my illegal activities. So why would God protect me from any harm when I was rolling with the Devil?

I can remember one morning when I was scheduled to appear in court. I sat in a holding cell with another inmate who was waiting to see the same judge. The man in the cell with me asked me how much I weighed? I told him I weighed 190 pounds. He told me that's how much he used to weigh. The man in front of me looked like an anorexic and weighed about 125 pounds. I asked him what happened to him. He told me he was addicted to crack cocaine and that it had destroyed him and his family. He said he stole from his parents, who kicked him out of their home. Then, he moved in with his grandmother and stole from her as well. Hearing his story, I realized what I had done. I had contributed to the destruction of his family and to those of many others. I had become a menace to society, and I hated the person I had become. I had become a version of my father.

I told myself then that I would never contribute to anything that would hurt another human being again. I needed to change my life, but how? I began to attend Bible study groups and, in 1993, I turned my life over to Jesus Christ, accepting him as my Lord and savior. I did not know if I could ever be forgiven, but I was certainly going to try.

I understood that, even though I'd become a Christian, I still had a sentence to complete and that I wasn't sitting in prison with a bunch of angels. I had my struggles, fights and prison riots, but now I knew I wasn't alone. I began to have a relationship with Jesus Christ, speaking to him day and night.

It was shortly after becoming a Christian that I ran into an old acquaintance from the street. It was a guy named Marky, and I hadn't seen him in about four or five years.

Marky had been a juvenile delinquent and was now facing charges for theft and robberies as an adult. He was sitting in prison and he was surprised to see me, as he told me that he didn't even know I was in jail. Very few people knew where I was or that I had been in prison for the last three-plus years.

Marky was still in contact with many of my old friends from elementary school and junior high, including Bridget and her younger sister Janet. He told me he had just been to Janet's wedding a few months earlier, and he said he could call Bridget to say hello. He called and then I got on the phone, and she was shocked to hear my voice and to know I was sitting next to Marky in jail.

We spoke for a few minutes and made plans for a visit, but before ending our call she asked if there was anyone I would like to see who would accompany her to see Marky and me. Bridget then suggested she could come over with Ivette, or another old friend, and asked me if I remembered Ivette from our junior high school. I said, "Of course I do," and told her it would be great to see Ivette and that there was a story behind how Ivette and I first met. Bridget said she would ask Ivette if she would accompany her on this church contact visit. But I doubted Ivette would come to a place like the one that I was in. In any case, I was happy to hear from an old friend and if she came to see us with Ivette, even better.

It was a couple of weeks later that Bridget convinced Ivette to accompany her to visit us. Bridget, who was one of Ivette's best friends, told her where I was and asked if she remembered me. Ivette said she did and was saddened to hear where I had ended up. Ivette, although sorry to hear what had happened to me, was not sad enough that she would not want to step into a jail to visit someone she hadn't seen in over a decade.

Ivette had left that junior high where I had last seen her and had graduated from La Salle, a Catholic high school, in 1987. Ivette had never visited anyone in jail or even known a convicted felon. But Bridget insisted that they come to see me, and it caught Ivette's imagination when she told her that I had said there was a story behind meeting Ivette; she didn't know that story.

Ivette was the cute girl who had caught my eye in my cousin's yearbook after my mother's murder when I moved in with my aunt and cousins. Ivette is the same girl who I accidentally kissed on the lips at the field day event in June of 1983. Ivette and I had gotten to know each other a little better when I was in the seventh grade and she was in ninth grade at Glades Junior High.

Ivette finally accepted the invitation to visit me in jail on April 7, 1993. The day of the visit, though, was a rainy Miami day and Ivette called Bridget to cancel because of the bad weather. Bridget, thank God, insisted they come. She convinced Ivette that she could not back out now that we were waiting. Ivette finally gave in and showed up to the visitation that evening. Ivette had no clue how the course of her life would change on that particular day.

At the end of our visitation, which was approximately an hour, I asked if I could give her a call afterwards to catch up and she said, "Yes." Man! That choice changed both our lives forever. I called Ivette the following day and proceeded to tell her about the story of how we met. I asked if she remembered our accidental kiss and she said of course. I also finally revealed I had found her in my cousin's 1980 and 1981 school yearbooks. Ivette and I fell in love soon after, and she made the sacrifice to wait out the remainder of my sentence, which was a little over seven years. Ivette has remained in my life ever since, more than three decades later.

As Ivette and I continued speaking over the phone and waiting for the appellate court to resolve my case, Ivette knew I would be heading back to Texarkana to finish my federal sentence. Eventually the appellate court decided in favor of the prosecutor and the motion to suppress was denied. The kilo of cocaine which Moose the dog had sniffed out was back in play. By this time I had already been sitting in Miami for thirty months, not six as my attorney had previously said. Had I resolved this case in six months, Ivette and I would not have reunited and I would not have the life I have today. The State of Florida eventually offered me a plea of five years and I accepted. Now I would have to wait for the Federal Marshals to take me back into the federal system.

It was now February 1994, and I remember one morning waking up after a dream of seeing my cousin Gregorio, looking down at me, standing in front of his cell on the fourth floor of a tier. This dream stuck with me because I hadn't seen him in fourteen years and I remember my father telling me about the hitmen going after him four times. And failing to kill him.

Shortly after the dream, I was standing on the second level of my unit when another inmate, Carlos Betancourt, walked up to me and told me, "A friend of your father is downstairs and is coming into our unit." I was shocked. I had met Carlos Betancourt in jail and he was from Colombia. We were in the same unit for months and he had never mentioned he knew my father.

As we were both standing there together, the man he spoke of walked into the unit and I immediately recognized him. Carlos Z was his name. He had lost a lung and had a very raspy voice. I first met Carlos Z in 1978 when I was eight years old. My mother had gone to see him in an apartment in Coral Gables for business. I remembered meeting him a few times as a child. I said to Carlos Betancourt, "Yes, I remember him."

Carlos Z was given a bottom floor one-man cell, and I walked down to greet him. I knew he wouldn't recognize me, but would definitely remember my parents. When I walked in his cell, he was sitting putting his things away and I said in Spanish, "Carlos, do you remember me?" Carlos Z said, "No." I said I am Maruja's son and I mentioned my father as well. Carlos Z immediately stood up and gave me a hug, telling me how lovely my mother was. Then he asked, "How is your father?" I told him he was fine and that we could call him on the phone to say hello.

He then asked me about Ignacio Rivas Junior, and I asked, "Why are you asking me about him?" He said he had maintained contact with Junior and had made millions with him back in the 1980s and that they still spoke by phone. Ignacio had actually opened up a modeling agency in Miami Beach after his release from federal prison. I told Carlos Z about the forty-two keys of coke that Junior had stolen from my father and that we had never heard from him again. Carlos Z said he didn't know about that, but that he could put him on the phone as well.

Later that afternoon, I called my father in Colombia with Carlos Z and they spoke for less than a minute, saying their hellos and goodbyes. Carlos Z spent the next two weeks with me in that unit before being transferred back to the Federal Marshals. I eventually was picked up by the Federal Marshals and sent to a federal holding facility in Miami to wait for the Federal Marshals' plane to make a pickup and take me back to Texarkana, Texas.

After three days back in Miami, I flew on the Marshals' plane, which was almost full of federal inmates, and we made our first stop in Atlanta to pick up more inmates. I was sitting near the front of the plane by myself in my row, waiting for the inmates to finish boarding from the tail end of the plane. As I looked to my right, to my astonishment, I saw my cousin Gregorio, who was shackled, walk past me.

I immediately called out to him. He looked to his left and nodded at me as he was placed in the row in front of me. Gregorio sat down but didn't look back. I called out to him again and asked him if he remembered me. He turned around and nodded his head, "Yes," then looked forward again.

Since he didn't continue with the conversation, I figured that he didn't want to speak to me because of the falling out with my father. Then, as I finished that thought, he turned around and asked, "How's Bianella doing?" I said she was fine, that she was a nurse and was married. I said to him, "Gregorio, when the plane takes off, let's both ask to go to the bathroom, and when we come back to our seats, let's sit on the same row so we can speak." And so we did.

When we came back, I could see the scar near his eye and on his neck. I asked him, "So what the hell happened?" Gregorio looked at me in surprise. "What happened! Do you know who did this to me?" as he pointed to his face! I told him that I did, and then he told me how and why. I told him I only knew my father's version of the story.

But then Gregorio proceeded to tell me his story, and it was almost the same as my father's, except in his version he wasn't trying to steal the merchandise. Gregorio said he was trying to negotiate with my father and to have my father continue supplying him in California. He went on to say my father took advantage of him and never paid him. That he was handling hundreds of thousands of dollars, and he would only pay him a couple hundred bucks here and there. Then, he proceeded to tell me in detail about all of the failed attempts on his life as we flew to El Reno, Oklahoma, to collect more inmates.

I then told Gregorio about Carlos Z, whom I had just run into a couple of weeks earlier.

Gregorio, shocked, replied, "What were you doing speaking to him?"

I said, "Why? Carlos walked into my unit, and I recognized him from the old days. We spent two weeks together in the same unit."

Gregorio then told me, "But he's the one who killed your mother!"

I was confused and shocked. I said, "That's not what my father told me. My father told me it was someone else, that it was Fernando, El Monje, and his sister Emma, La Monja."

Gregorio then explained that he had heard it was Carlos Z who had done the hit. Gregorio had run into El Rey Moncada at the Dadeland Mall, which is a huge mall in Kendall. El Rey, as Moncada was called, was a heavy hitter and well connected in Medellin. He was a close friend from childhood of Carlos Z. Gregorio said El Rey had heard that Gregorio was asking around about my mother and Kiko's murders. El Rey confirmed that Carlos Z did the hit, but then said, in a threatening manner, to leave it alone.

Gregorio and I arrived in El Reno and took a bus ride to Federal Correctional Institution, El Reno. FCI El Reno is a medium-security federal prison for about 1,000 male inmates, originally built in 1933. As we were being strip searched, I could see all the keloid scars over Gregorio's torso and back. He had survived four assassination attempts, been shot a total of thirteen times, completed a nine-year sentence in the federal system and was now on his way to serve a life sentence for the murder of his ex-girlfriend in California.

When we received our supplies and were waiting in line to be assigned to our cells, I told Gregorio, "Let's speak to the guards on duty tomorrow and ask to be placed in the same cell together." We were approximately forty inmates checking in and we were waiting for the correctional officers to call our names. They did, and they called Gregorio's name and my name together. We had been assigned to the same cell without us even asking, and we couldn't believe it. What were the chances I would run into him on the Federal Marshals' plane where he would be sat in the row in front of me and now be placed in the same cell together?

We spoke the whole night, sharing stories and remembering the old times. The following morning, I walked down from the fourth-tier cell where we were assigned in order to make a call to my sister to tell her who I was with. As I was speaking to her, I looked up at Gregorio, who was looking down from the fourth tier by his cell. I said to my sister, "Nella, remember the dream I had of Gregorio?" She said, "Yes," I said, "I'm looking up at him right now." The dream I had weeks earlier was live and in front of me. I told

Nella all that had happened the day before and that we were now in the same cell together. I knew who killed our mother and Kiko.

Gregorio and I spent a few more days together before I would be shipped out to Texarkana. Shortly after arriving in Texarkana, I received a letter from Marco's mother with a letter from Marco. Marco, who had been my friend in high school, and who I first got into the drug dealing business with, had been arrested in Boston, Massachusetts, with nine other Colombians after smuggling one thousand kilos of cocaine. He was sentenced to ten years in federal prison for his involvement in that crime, and was designated to FCI Jessup in Georgia. In his letter, he wrote to me that he was being sent to the satellite camp in a few months and that he would be doing, in his words, "a Houdini Act" and escape back to Colombia.

Once Marco arrived, we spoke over the phone, and he asked me when I would be sent to the federal camp. I said by the following year, but that I had no plans to escape. I was now with Ivette, and we were very much in love and making plans for our future, which did not include being on the run in Colombia. Ivette, as much as she loved me, would never do such a thing, and I, at that point in my prison life, would never even think about it. My life of crime was behind me and that's where it was staying.

I was eventually sent to the federal camp at Eglin Air Force Base in April of 1995. My job at the camp was working at a tire shop, with ten-ton dump trucks. Visitations were much easier as Ivette would drive up to see me as often as she could–but definitely not as much as we wanted. My sister and Tony would come up with Ivette as well.

My sister had been dating Tony for a few years now and had plans to get married. Tony was my best friend and was the only friend in our group from junior high who never got involved in the drug business. His parents were also from Colombia and worked an honest living in Miami, with their own import and export business. His family showed me what an honest living looked like. Remember, my father told me, "In this country you can't make a single dollar legally," but Tony's parents were doing it.

Tony had started dating my sister Nella in eighth grade in 1984. The same year my sister and I went to live with our father. When my sister broke up with Tony, he joined our group of friends, becoming one my best and closest friends to this day, forty years later. Tony and Nella started dating again in 1991 and have been committed to each other ever since.

Marco, true to his word, did his Houdini act and escaped from prison and made his way to Colombia. Soon after arriving in Bogota, he got back into the game. On July 21, 1996, I was contacted by my prison counselor to call Tony. I called Tony and he told me Marco was dead. Marco had been killed by the police in Colombia in a shootout. What I learned was that Marco had gone to a restaurant with a woman and two bodyguards. He apparently got into a fight with the waiter and there was a shootout. When the police arrived, they killed Marco and his bodyguards, leaving their bodies riddled with bullets. Marco Aurelio Gomez died, leaving his son Marco Jr. and his wife Angelica behind. I saw what my future could have been, but was determined to not let it ever happen. When I heard the news about Marco, I still had about four years left of my sentence.

As time went on, Ivette and I continued our conversations with hopes and dreams of our future together. They say that time flies when you're having fun. The opposite is true as well: time runs at a snail's pace when you're miserable.

Two years later, in June 1998, Ivette, Nella and Tony drove up to see me and brought along my little sister Tatiana, who was now eight years old. Tatiana was born two weeks after I went to prison in December 1989, and I had never met her. Nella was getting married to Tony, and Tatiana would be in their wedding party as their flower girl. I was excited for my sister and Tony; they were living their dream. Nella was getting married to the love of her life and had a baby on the way. I was truly happy to see that after all that had happened for her: she was finally going to see some happiness.

Ivette, in the same month my sister was getting married, was making her own plans and moved up from Miami to Fort Walton Beach, Florida, in the northwest corner of the state, close to Alabama, to be closer to me and to continue our weekly visitations. We were super excited. Ivette had sold everything, including her furniture, and had rented a small apartment near the camp.

On June 30, 1998, when I came back from working on the Air Force Base, I was contacted by my prison counselor and was told to call my sister, Nella. My stomach sank; what now? When I called Nella, she told me, "Alain, our father has been killed in Colombia. He was murdered this morning."

I remember thinking, "Has this really happened again?" It had indeed happened again, and I couldn't say I wasn't surprised. My father was murdered by hitmen after dropping off his wife, Doris, at work. Doris told us that she had seen two guys on motorcycles entering the valley where she worked in Guatica, Colombia, and two more guys on motorcycles at the bottom of the valley entering town. When my father was heading back to the farm, he was gunned down by the men on motorcycles at the top of the valley.

After I hung up with my sister, I went to my bunk and cried. I couldn't remember the last time I cried. I mean, I didn't even cry when my mother and Kiko were murdered, and I was eleven. I don't know why I cried for this man; I didn't love my father. He was a terrible human being that didn't deserve anyone's love. My father was a drug dealer, a thief, an abusive father and husband, a child molester and a murderer.

I mean, he told me himself he had killed Carlos, Doris's boyfriend, and had tried to kill my cousin Gregorio four times. My father had even told me when I was seventeen that he didn't love me, that he had only loved me as a child. Who says shit like that? My father definitely didn't deserve my tears and so I never cried for him again. I truly felt guilty for not crying for my own mother. I think my tears that night were just a culmination of the tragic events that had happened in my twenty-eight years of life.

Ivette and I were happier now that we could see each other weekly, and sometimes my boss at work, for a small fee, would let me walk away and spend time with Ivette. I was even able to visit her new apartment. This only lasted a few months because, on October 19, 1998, I went to see Ivette as planned and was turned in by another inmate who I'd thought was a friend, Barry Goodman. Barry had been caught with contraband in the camp and had cooperated with the lieutenant and turned me in. I was caught while trying to meet Ivette and charged with attempted escape.

I was sent to FCI Marianna in Marianna, Florida, to finish my sentence. Ivette would have to drive two hours each way to visit me on the weekends. I also met up there with a longtime friend, KC, whom I had known since grade six. We became cellmates and we would talk about what we would do when we got out. I dared to hope I had a future. I finished my sentence at Marianna FCI, completing ten years, six months and eight days. I was twenty-nine years old.

I remember the morning of my release praying to my Lord Jesus to please help me and guide me. I prayed for a new life with Ivette and a career to support her and a family with. I asked God to bless me and Ivette and to open doors that I knocked on.

Ivette picked me up after waiting seven years, two months and twenty days. What seemed like an eternity. It really was a miracle in my eyes that Ivette was able to hang on all those years, especially since we had never been a couple in the free world. I saw many relationships and marriages not survive one year, much less seven. Ivette and I were finally free on the other side of the fence with no restrictions and free to begin our lives together with God's blessing. We were truly in disbelief driving down the Florida Turnpike to the halfway house in Dania Beach, Florida, a small town south of Fort Lauderdale where I spent ten days. Ivette had moved down from Fort Walton Beach to Boca Raton, Florida, almost a year prior, settling in a one-bedroom apartment ready for the both of us. Ivette and I started our lives together as one, and we had a very easy transition. We couldn't believe it. All those years of life behind bars were now behind us. We were now looking at the rest of our lives in front of us, and going forward with God's blessing.

CHAPTER 8: Starting Over

Alain remembers...
Following my release, Ivette and I reunited with my sister and Tony, who were now pregnant with their second child, Dassio. Nella had already given birth to Isabella, a beautiful baby girl. The first month of release was very exciting; Ivette finally introduced me to her sister, Ivonne, and her brother-in-law, Eric, who is an attorney in Palm Beach County. Ivonne and Eric were very welcoming and made me feel at home. I can only imagine their thoughts of me. I mean, it can't be easy knowing that your sister and sister-in-law has fallen in love with a man in prison and is bringing him over for Thanksgiving. I could only hope that they knew Ivette to be a great human being with a good heart and could only pray that this was all part of God's plan. We enjoyed a wonderful Thanksgiving and I felt very welcomed into Ivette's family. A few weeks later, in December of 2000, I asked Ivette to marry me. She said yes, and we set a date for October of 2001.

Shortly afterwards, my old cellmate KC got released from prison as well. I remember asking him what his plans were now that he was free, and he told me his brother-in-law owned a land survey company in Miami and thought that he should consider getting into the real estate business as a property appraiser. I asked him, "What is a property appraiser?" He said he didn't know, but that it sounded like a good career.

KC and I signed up for real estate school and became property appraisers in June 2001.

While I was in real estate school, Ivette surprised me with the great news that she was pregnant. I was scared, but our dreams were coming true: we were getting married in a few months and now we were pregnant. I was broke, but very happy and following God's plan. Ivette and I got married in August of 2001. We ended up having to move up the wedding date to August because of the pregnancy.

I started my career in October of 2001 when the Real Estate Appraiser Board accepted my license after holding a hearing over my criminal conviction. The Real Estate Appraisal Board decided to give me a chance after listening to my story. I told them I was nineteen years old when I went to prison, that I had spent ten years there and that I was now married and expecting a child. I told them I had left that criminal life behind me and was ready to start my life in this new career. If they would allow me that chance.

I had already found a job near my apartment, thanks to God. Every door I knocked on was open. The first call I made out of the Yellow Pages was to an appraisal firm that hired me right out of Real Estate School. You would think I was lucky; I know I wasn't. I never was. God's plan was playing out.

A few months later, in February 2002, my daughter Alanna was born, a beautiful baby girl. I was now a father, but what kind of father would I be? I knew I wouldn't be like my father; this child would be loved with all of my heart and soul and would never be placed in danger. I wanted to be the type of father who told his kids that he loves them every day. I always do. What a gift she was and is to Ivette and me.

Ivette and I had another beautiful healthy baby girl, Nina, in June 2005. Two blessings from God. Ivette and I promised each other we wouldn't tell the girls about my past until they were both out of high school–and we kept that commitment.

It was around 2005 when Nella and I had a conversation about bringing one of our half-sisters, Maya, to live with us. The eldest of Doris's daughters, Alicia, was born in Colombia, and although she had US residence, she had lost it. Maya, our second half-sister, had grown tired of living on a farm in Colombia, and came to live with Ivette and me. But Maya got homesick and went back to the farm in Colombia. And now, Maya wanted to return to the US; she was born in Miami and was a US citizen. She was now an adult, twenty-one years old.

Even if Maya had bailed on us before, Nella decided, after thinking about it, that she would take Maya in for our father and would let her stay with Tony and her in their home. Those words didn't sit well with me. I told her that if she were to do it, then it should be on the basis of helping our sister in pursuit of a new life here in the US. Besides, I said, "What happened with mom wasn't clear to me." Nella asked, "What do you mean?"

"Nella," I said. "Let's put everything we know on the table, as if this were an episode of NBC's Dateline, where our father would have been a prime suspect. Dad had a mistress who was our cousin, and she had a baby ten days after the murders! I mean, what the hell!?"

"What do we know?" I continued. "We know he murdered people. We know he killed Carlos, Doris's boyfriend, and he tried to kill Gregorio several times."

"So would it be too far-fetched that after our mother shot at him for spitting in her face at the house he would be angry enough to kill her for it? He literally told me a couple times in anger he would put two bullets in my head. I think enough is enough. He even had Doris staying at his sister Octavia's house in Medellin while she was pregnant. That alone is a huge betrayal to my mother by her own sister-in-law."

Now my sister and I began to ask ourselves if this is all true, then who else knows?

We had to assume that all adults on both sides of the family knew.

Nella and I scheduled an appointment with the homicide detectives in Miami-Dade to try to find out more. Before the meeting, my sister spoke with my father's sister, Yesenia, and told her what we were thinking and planning.

Nella and I then had our meeting with a homicide detective who brought out a box with our mother and Kiko's case file.

The original detective on the case had died, so we met with another detective, an older white man. He told us that, normally, there would have been a lot more boxes, but our mother was killed in 1982, a year when there had been more than seven hundred homicides and resources were stretched too thin to thoroughly investigate each case. Many of them were still unsolved.

We spoke with the detective for about an hour. We explained why we were there and told him about our suspicions. And when we told him what we knew, he informed us that our father was a suspect and asked where he was. We told him our father had been murdered in Colombia in 1998. He shook his head and his response was, "Well, it's a cold case now."

Nella and I left that meeting convinced and clear about what had happened to our mother and uncle. I later called my cousins and uncle in Medellin and asked them if they knew anything about my mother and Kiko's murders and who they believed had killed them. They came clean and told me that everything I had suspected based on what I had been told was true. They had always known my father had murdered their aunt and uncle. In Miami, my father's sister Yesenia was waiting to hear from Nella about the meeting with the homicide detective. Nella confirmed with her what we suspected as well, and my aunt began to cry, telling my sister that they also suspected our father, but didn't ask him about it. She said he was their oldest brother and didn't want to believe that their own brother would be capable of doing such a thing.

This was a lot for my sister and me to take in and finally accept. My sister and I were the only ones who had believed our father's lies. When you're eleven years old and endured all we went through, we just simply believed him. Or maybe deep inside I didn't want to believe it was possible, but it was, and it did happen.

My sister and I continued living our lives for the most part as normally as we could. My sister had built a beautiful family and by this time already had three children. She was a wonderful, caring and well respected Delivery and Labor nurse. I had a gorgeous wife who had given me two beautiful girls. Nella focused on her work and her family and I focused on mine.

I found a way to release stress thanks to my youngest daughter Nina, who wanted to do karate. At the time UFC, Ultimate Fighting Championship, with mixed martial arts, was hugely popular. But I felt Jiu-jitsu would be great for my girls to take up to learn self-defense. Nina and Alanna joined the American Top Team and started practicing Brazilian Jiu-jitsu.

On their first day of training, their coach and owner of the gym approached Ivette and me and asked what the girls thought about the training session. I told him that they had given me a thumbs-up. The coach then asked me, "What about you, why don't you and your wife give it a try?" I told him that after years of lifting weights I had three herniated discs and didn't know if I could. The coach said he had four herniated discs, leaving me with no excuses. So my training began in 2012, and as for Ivette, she tried Jiu-jitsu but decided she liked kickboxing instead.

My coach, Marcos DaMatta, owns the gym in West Palm Beach and is a trainer for American Top Team at Coconut Creek, Florida. Marcos, known as "Parrumpa", was about forty years old at the time I met him, and he is not a big man at five feet four inches and 145 pounds, but he is powerful. He started his Brazilian Jiu-jitsu training in 1987 at Carlson Gracie Main Academy in Copacabana, Rio de Janeiro, Brazil. He has won all his belts from Grand Master Carlson Gracie and was promoted to Black Belt in December of 1997 by Grand Master Carlson Gracie himself. He has won all major titles in BJJ and is considered one of the best light featherweights of the 1990s and early 2000s.

Marcos moved to the US in 2002 to start the Brazilian Jiu-jitsu program at American Top Team. He became a Mixed Martial Arts coach and is now one of the most successful MMA coaches in the world, having coached UFC, Professional Fighters Leagues, Bellator (an MMA promotion with a Latin name meaning "warrior"), and PRIDE World Championships, which is the Japanese version of MMA.

Marcos also has his own American Top Team Affiliate in West Palm Beach, Florida.

I was hooked. I asked Marcos how long it would take me to earn a black belt. He said it would take about ten years. The same amount of time I had been in prison, I thought. But this was a much better use of my time. Ivette was surprised that I would want to attempt this with my injured back. "You have to be careful, you're getting older," she reminded me. She also wanted to know whether, if I was going to take Jiu-jitsu, I was eventually going to compete. I told her I didn't think so.

So I started my classes. My daughters did Jiu-jitsu for about eight months. Then they stopped and pursued other sports, but I continued and began competing and I am still at it. I'm proud to say I have earned my Black Belt in Brazilian Jiu Jitsu and continue training to this day. Ivette comes with me to support me and is my biggest fan. She's always my cheerleader at every match in which I compete.

So you could say that Jiu-jitsu started because of the family I had created, and then Jiu-jitsu became a family in and of itself. Engaging with this martial art allows me to relieve the stresses of the family that I came from, stresses that I didn't even know I had until I started doing Jiu-jitsu. Stresses that nearly killed me, and from which I had become a better man.

Nella remembers...

When Alain was released from prison on June 27, 2000, I was pregnant with my second child, a son, who would be born in September 2000. For the last twelve years, I had imagined this day of freedom. At Christmas time, I always get emotional, because I remember always singing that song from Mariah Carey, "All I Want for Christmas". I remember just always wishing over the course of twelve Christmases that I wanted my brother to be with me and to be a free man.

In my vision I was outside of the jail, watching the doors open as we ran up to each other and reunited.

But "Life" happened. I was married and expecting a baby and Alain had found love. Ivette and he had been committed to each other for the last seven years, and it was Ivette who was waiting for him when those doors opened. They were happy and very much in love. She had sacrificed years of her own life waiting for him, and now it was time for them to start their new life together as a free couple.

Ivette and I had driven together a few times to the prison. It was eight to twelve hours of driving. I would fall asleep as she drove; other times, Tony would join us. We were a trio, and Ivette was fun to be with. She has a great sense of humor and liked to keep things light.

I finally went to visit my brother at the halfway house in which he was living. We were very happy to be together again. The next time I saw him was in my apartment. My daughter Isabella was a year-and-a-half old, and I was now eight months pregnant with my son. It was nighttime. My husband Tony was with me, and somebody knocked at the door. It was my brother, and I remember being ecstatic to see him walk through our door. I ran and I hugged him, pulling him into my big pregnant belly. He was really skinny, and I just wanted to feed him.

It was so nice to be together because it was the first time Alain was going to be able to be part of a family birth. He had missed the birth of my daughter, but he was going to be here for my son, so it was a dream come true for us.

When I went to have my baby, Alain promised to be there. He was running late, and my C-section surgery was scheduled at eight in the morning. I thought he wasn't going to make it. But because I worked at the hospital where I was giving birth, my colleagues let Alain in when he arrived and allowed him to come all the way into the OR. He gave me a hug and kiss, and we video-captured the moment of Alain holding his nephew shortly after he came into the world.

For those with "normal" families, we take it for granted that they will be present at our big life events. But for me, this was the first time I had somebody from my immediate family with me for a birth. Alain was here, and it felt to me like my family had finally come to a point of normalcy.

And then a year later he and Ivette got pregnant. They were making up for lost time. They got married and had two girls. And he came out of prison like a lion ready to make up for lost time and to work and make a living. He was ready.

During all those years in prison, Tony and Alain spoke of business ideas for Alain to start when he was released. I think Tony was influential because he never did drugs; he was honest and loyal. Tony had become a full time realtor, and he and Alain talked of appraisals and other real estate possibilities. I just fell in love with my husband Tony even more, as he was such a good friend to Alain. They would talk every day about the possibilities for making money out there in the market. They would talk about houses, appraisals, and even the stock market. They still do. They speak often, even several times a week.

I was very grateful for that because I was working and raising three kids. I was in a good place. I was happy and I was focusing on my children, my husband, and my brother. And then, my brother was raising questions about our mother's murder, so we started talking about our mother.

We went to the homicide department in Miami. We asked the police about our mother's case. I wanted to know what information or evidence they had. They came in with a box of evidence and they listened to us, and I could see that the officers had empathy for us. The detective who spoke to us was a middle-aged white man of medium stature. He spoke to us in English. But in his eyes I could see he felt terrible. He felt very sad.

He and the other detective actually apologized to us for not having more boxes of evidence. We asked why hadn't the investigation continued? One detective stated that, back in 1982, they were understaffed and had a very high rate of homicides. More than 700 in that one year. Two a day.

"Due to the crime wave in the early 1980s with drug dealers stealing from each other, your mother and Francisco's murders were probably seen as a drug deal gone bad, since your family was from Colombia." The detective stated that he wasn't a detective then, but his opinion was that there were just too many cases to follow and not enough police to deal properly with it all. They kind of just left it as drug dealers dispensing their own justice.

And me, being who I am today, I spoke my mind. This was a good moment for me to speak, because I told them they owed justice to two innocent children, and that we didn't choose this life-changing event.

"We didn't choose our parents. But after our mother was murdered, we really needed somebody to look out for us and find justice for us. But you never bothered to look. If you had just come back to speak with us, you would have found out that ten days later my half-sister was born, and our father moved back to Colombia to live with our murdered mother's niece and their daughter. You would have known then. And that alone was motive in and of itself."

They did tell us that our father had been the number-one suspect from the very beginning. When our father found out about the murders, he drove to our house, and then he turned his car around and drove straight to the lawyer Nathan Diamond's office, which was forty-five minutes away. Any other husband would run to the site and try to find out what happened. Our father went to see his lawyer, and they found that suspicious.

All of the things were in a box: files, notes and photos. The detective took out some pictures. I know my brother had asked to see pictures of the scene, and the detective said, "No, no, I don't think that's a good idea." I agree.

The adult I am now understands this better, but back then, Alain and I were struggling with trauma. I'm studying even more now about trauma. Trauma affects us, affects our psyche; it changes our behaviors and our reactions to events. And as a nurse, I know, there are things you cannot "unsee."

We then told the detective everything we knew about the murders and left with the knowledge that what we felt had happened was true.

I was upset. My whole world was upside down. I couldn't sleep. And it was hard for me to go to work. I was very angry. I just kept going around in circles trying to figure out this shocking revelation. I didn't want to go to therapy. But I knew that I had to go speak with a psychologist to discover how I could find and accept the truth.

I had seen a therapist before, when I was twenty-one. It was through one of the doctors I worked for, Dr. Dimino. I was taking care of his children, and his family were very kind to me. He had a sister-in-law who was young like me and recommended a therapist, Rosalind Shea.

It was a 45-minute drive from where I lived to her office. The first time I met with her, she asked me, "Why are you here?" I told her, "I don't know. But my friend said I should see you. She really thinks that you can help me. I really don't think I need anything." I remember Rosalind just smiled at me, and told me, "In this room, we hug. You don't like to hug?" I said, "Well, I don't know." I realized then that I just wasn't accustomed to this, to hugging, to affection. And so I learned to hug and to be open to that in her office.

I also recall Rosalind asking me, "How much can you afford?" I stayed quiet, and she said, "Can you give me $10?" And I said, "Yes, I can do $10," because I only had $18 to my name after a paycheck. I realized now she was giving me power and independence and dignity, and she was being so generous about doing so.

Rosalind Shea taught me about myself. She was the first person to tell me, Doris is not your friend. I was still talking and sending her money and believing everything that Doris would tell me. And Rosalind was the first one to introduce me to how my different emotions were working on me. I remember her saying, "You have sadness, fear, anger, and you have gravitated to sadness. You become very comfortable there. But now you need to learn how to feel anger. How to feel happy, how to feel fun."

And I thought it was crazy, but she helped me come to terms with myself. I even got very comfortable with anger. Then, Rosalind wanted me to learn how to have fun. I still push myself to do that, because I tend not to be the fun one. So my kids laugh at me when I act silly, and they love it when I do, because I go out of character when I do something silly.

Rosalind really helped me grow and learn more about myself, and to push myself forward and learn how to say no, because I didn't know how to say no. God forbid, I would speak my mind! Rosalind would say, "It's okay, baby, when you're angry, you have to show it with your face!" At the end of a year, she pronounced, "Okay, baby, we're done." But I didn't want these sessions to end.

I remember she asked me when we began what my goals were. I told her I don't want to be afraid of my dad anymore. I know he's going to be killed. I just knew it, and I don't want any regrets. At the therapy a year later, I learned how to speak to my dad without trembling. I was not afraid of him anymore. I spoke my mind and he came to respect me, and to admire me.

My father even told me, a year before he died, to stop sending Doris money. "Don't believe her. She's lying. She is just crying wolf." I had to work three jobs to send her the money she said she needed; my father was telling me she did not really need it.

My father and I would even sit down and have conversations, and I would tell him that the things he had done were wrong, and that there is a God. "Aren't you afraid?" I asked. And he would be very frank with me and say, "I deal with things my way. Here on Earth, money and power rule, and I will be at His mercy when my time comes."

But now, knowing that my father had my mother killed, and Uncle Kiko, too, I went back into therapy. I gave myself three months. I was not going to be dealing with this for the next decade and besides, therapy was expensive, and it wasn't covered by my insurance.

So I found a wonderful therapist named Susan and I told her that she had three months to sort me out. "I just need you to give me the tools to put this in order so I can figure it out and let go of it. I have a good life. I have a great husband. I have three beautiful kids, and they deserve the best of me right now. They have the worst of me because I'm in prison. I'm in the ground, buried with my father. He has control of every emotion and every thought. I'm a prisoner. I need to figure this shit out and I need to be able to let it go." So I told the therapist, "You have three months, and I will do everything that I have to do."

Susan agreed. She was a very kind, very maternal woman, and she said that it was going to be painful. And it was. Painful for me emotionally, and painful for my husband. It hurt me to see him cry for me. I didn't want to give him pain, and I was hurting him. But at the end of it, I had walked through the flames and had come out for the better. I was able to let go of the past, or the most painful part of it. It was a process. Now I was prepared to deal with the truth.

I think I realized I was finally ready when I confronted my aunt, Yesenia, and I asked, "Did you know your brother killed our mother?" And she immediately started crying, and said, "Please don't tell my children." That, to me, was a confession.

Everybody knew that our father had murdered our mother except us.

At that time, I would think about O.J. Simpson. I would think about his son and daughter. Their father, O.J., killed their mother, Nicole. They probably didn't believe he had done so because even though the evidence was right in front of them, just like us, with the evidence right in front of us, we didn't really see it. Because your psyche doesn't allow you to see it.

I would see the O.J. trial on TV while my brother was still in prison. When O.J. was acquitted, many people, especially white people, were furious. We all knew he had committed those murders, and that justice had not prevailed. However, part of me felt like I was getting set free when he was freed, because I almost felt like O.J. was substituting for my father. I empathized with O.J. because of that, and I felt for his two children, thinking that they could not lose their father too, having lost their mother. I was looking at it from the perspective of the boy and the girl, from the perspective of Alain and me.

This is the second thing in my transformation when the truth was yet again confirmed, but this time by my own memory. One day, I was sitting there, and a powerful memory came to me.

I told you part of this story earlier, but at the time, I did not understand it; and yet it was important to know, to remember. I was a child then, but thinking about it now as an adult, it all became very clear to me. It was probably a month before our mother died. My mother, father and I were in the living room, and I was sitting on the floor with my mother. My father was sitting on the sofa. He was drinking and telling us about the land he had just bought in Colombia. He had bought a farm, with horses and cattle, and he told us that all of these things were a sign of how important he was in Colombia.

I was more interested in the horses than his ego, so I said, "When are we going? I want to go ride horses!" My father replied, "You will go soon." But then he pointed to my mother and said, "But she will not see it."

I remembered at that age, when I was eleven years old, thinking, "Why did you say that?" But suddenly, that memory connected with my adult self, and I knew. My father had said that to my mother because he knew he was going to kill her. That, to me, was the answer. That, to me, was really when I knew he had done it because he had told me.

That was, as they say, my "aha" moment.

I had put it in the back of my mind, and thirty-four years later it came roaring back to life.

The truth had always been there, with me. Now I had seen it.

The most difficult thing for me to do was to let go of Doris, because she was still alive. Aunt Nubia told me years later she did not approve of her own daughter, of what Doris had done and had thrown her out. She even told her other daughter who had a house not to take Doris in. I appreciate that my aunt told me this. I know she has had a hard life, losing her favorite sister, my mother, and her brothers Kiko and John. She also lost her older brother's support. There was never any reconciliation, and I am sorry for my aunt for that. She has been nothing but loving and warm-hearted to me.

I think it's easier to forgive somebody who's dead. I was angry with my mother, too. As a mother, I was asking myself why had she allowed this to happen? Why had she stayed with this man when I had begged her to leave?

When I became a nurse, I had to take classes in psychology and learn about depression and anxiety, but also about domestic violence. I understood my mom's psyche and her fears: I came to understand why she stayed with my father, why she didn't fight back. I also knew that they had a limited education; my father only finished grade four. Nor did they have worldly knowledge about stocks, investing and saving, and planning for the future of your children. They didn't do that.

But my mother provided for her family in Colombia. My mother bought a couple of houses in which one was used for our grandmother and Aunt Nubia to live in. She helped pay for her nieces and nephews to go to college. My father took back everything my mother bought for them–the house, everything. If he could have taken back their college education he would have. And the house I lived in was foreclosed, and I had to work three jobs in order to survive and put myself through school.

I'm not angry with my mom at all anymore, but I was for a while, as a woman; I was furious that she didn't leave my abusive father. But I realized now that it was psychological: she was bound to him. If she left, he would kill her. And she couldn't really leave him because she knew too much.

I was angry with my mom for a long time, and then with therapy and education, and through nursing, I've learned to forgive her. I've tried to honor her by being the best version I could be of her, and of myself.

With my father, I was angry that he had done this to us, and at what he had not done. I could count the times on one hand that he had said, "I love you" to me, or to any of us. And he would have to be drunk to say it. He was not a loving man.

One time I said to him, "Why can't you just love me like Lorena's dad? Why can't you be a little bit more like him?" My father was so angry at my request. "Don't you ever compare me to anybody! This is my way."

When I think back on the meeting with the police, the detective said our mother and Kiko's murders were still open, a cold case, waiting to be solved. But the mastermind was dead. They didn't propose any further detective work because they and we knew that our father had ordered the murders. But who were the men who pulled the trigger?

I don't know what to say about that. Part of me wanted to know who the two people were who murdered our mother and our uncle. I wanted to know what they looked like and see their faces, but at the same time I was scared because I did not want them to come back to hurt me and my family.

My kids want to go to Colombia and the country is a part of me. I love Colombia. It's beautiful and vibrant green and alive. Everyone is so welcoming. But I don't know if we should travel there because there are likely people in Colombia who still hold a grudge against our father. They could want to hurt me because of what our father did there. Our father hurt a lot of people. He killed our mother and her brother, his own brother-in-law. He killed people in his family and our mother's family; he killed strangers; he was a sociopathic murderer. I don't even know all of his transgressions. My sisters know some of it. But their mother Doris knows all of it.

I do not like Doris, nor do I trust her. She remains a selfish woman whom I have no relation to whatsoever. My sister Alicia got married and Doris got to be there, at her daughter's wedding. I had no parents at mine, but my little sister was my flower girl. My brother was in prison, my father was in Colombia, and my mother was murdered. Doris gets to be a grandmother and she gets to have her whole family with her. The injury continues because my children were denied the love of their grandmother.

I love my three sisters, but I have set boundaries to have a healthy sibling relationship. Our three sisters understand and know how we feel. They are innocent, just as we are innocent, of our parents' choices.

CHAPTER 9: Healing the Body

Nella speaks...

How did we cope with the pain of our history, the violence and lovelessness, and the terrible mystery of the murders which haunted our lives? Exercise has always been important for both my brother and me. We loved to play outside together when we were little, and we had no idea of what kind of trouble was coming our way. Those were the days when afternoons seemed to last forever, and all we could do was play them out.

By the time I was an adult and working three jobs, I was not getting much exercise. My friend, Thelma, who had paid for me to go to nursing school, was the one who got me onto the exercise track. She said, "Why don't you come by my house, and we'll go for a walk?" So we started walking together, and we would do charity walks for organizations like the March of Dimes, a non-profit that works to improve the health of mothers and babies. So we enjoyed our walks, and then one day she told me that she was planning on walking a marathon. Would I be interested in joining her?

I was interested. All I had done was to stay at home and read books, as books were my passport–and remain my passport–to knowledge, and to people I wouldn't otherwise meet, and to places I otherwise would not see. But they were not marathons.

I had thought about trying out running when I was in school, but I didn't follow through. Now Thelma was offering me a chance to go on a new journey, and I wanted to take it.

I didn't even train for this marathon! Every Tuesday, Thelma and I would go for long walks together, and I saved up some money and bought myself a pair of sneakers. I ran my first marathon, all 26.2 miles of it, on June 5, 1991.

It was in Miami, and the weather was gorgeous. I felt great after mile 22. I ran for my mother, I ran for my brother, I ran for my anger. I didn't realize how therapeutic it was just thinking about them while I was running and trying to process everything that happened to me–and to us. It was incredible to me because it was my greatest physical accomplishment so far in my life. Athletics had always been about my brother, because he was the one who excelled at everything physical. This was the first time that I realized I, too, could do something athletic. I mean, running a marathon is not a casual commitment.

More importantly, I learned that running was about the mind. I hadn't trained physically for this marathon (I know, rookie mistake!), so I had to rely on my mind to get me through those 26.2 miles and to release all those tensions and struggles that had built up through the years because of all that happened to me and to my family.

Ever since that first marathon I have run regularly to relieve the stresses of life, and to have the freedom to let my mind roam. Recently, my eldest daughter asked me if I would do a half-marathon with her. She had been having a hard time finding a job the year after she finished college, as the job market these days is a tough one for recent grads. So she wanted to do a half-marathon to raise her spirits and invited me to join her.

The last time I did a marathon was more than 20 years ago in 2003. I thought it would be nice to run it with her: the mother and daughter marathon. So we did. I successfully completed a half marathon with my daughter in March 2024. I've continued my running journey that began when I was 20, and as of last year, I started yoga, which I enjoy very much. I love the breathing and the stillness of it. Between the aerobic exercise of running and the calm that yoga brings, I am in a good physical place.

My brother Alain has always been athletic, and even though we're twins, we're very different in many ways. He takes risks where I am terrified of risks. I feel safest surrounded with rules and structure. I find that Alain needs Jiu-jitsu, which has become very therapeutic for him.

I have told Alain that we have both done a great job at becoming our strongest versions of ourselves. Even more important, we have grown to be kind, compassionate members of society.

Sometimes there will be triggers that bring back the past in a horrific flash. For me, if I see yellow police tape on the TV news, it's an automatic trigger. I'll be thinking about it all night, about what that tape means to me, and I know what those left behind will be waking up to.

Then I have to remind myself, yes, once I was affected by that tape; but it's not me this time. All I can do is pray for the souls of those to whom the tape now has meaning. It's very easy to get triggered by and then swallowed up in that memory. I share my triggers with Alain, so he knows these triggers are normal– and that they are going to pass. Alain and I did not come out of this unscarred. We both suffer from anxiety and PTSD, which can be triggered by tragic stories we see on the local news. My husband Tony knows when I'm anxious and processing something in my head because I'll start cleaning everything, and organizing and reorganizing the house. More so than usual. My great losses caused me to feel imminent danger all the time. I felt fear. Fear of losing my children, my husband, my home. My fears influenced my parenting style. They made me controlling, but slowly, thanks to Tony and Lorena's help, I learned to let go and trust God.

I eventually shared my story with our kids, and this helped them understand me better. I shared my vulnerability with them and they in turn grew to be more compassionate with us. To this day, my children are very much aware of life's fragility. They value their time with us, and they will not depart from our house before coming to us, looking us in the eye and giving us a hug. Because their greatest lesson came from me, when I ran out of that house at eleven years of age, to go on my field trip. And I turned back to give my mother a kiss. She gave me her blessing. But I didn't look in her eyes. And I never saw those eyes alive again.

I think that it was a good choice to tell them. Because it's my reality. I can't sugarcoat and make this world look beautiful and wonderful, and pain-free. I have to gently tell them the truth and how to manage it. It's better to teach them the tools of how to handle life's challenges than to put them in a protective bubble, because all bubbles eventually burst.

Alain speaks…

I had been looking for ways to test myself besides the weight training, which I had started with my cousin Juan when I was ten years old. I had always been close to my cousin even though he was ten years older than me. As a kid, he had introduced me to boxing, weight training and the martial arts, in particular, Taekwondo. I'm grateful to Juan for introducing me to all of these things.

I have done weight training my whole life. I had begun to do Spartan and Tough Mudder Races, which are very exciting but only happen a few times a year, and the running was killing my back.

When I started Jiu-jitsu it came at the right time for me. It was humbling: I weighed 220 pounds and stood almost six feet tall, but I was getting my ass handed to me by guys 50 pounds lighter. I would see my coach, Parrumpa, who's five feet four inches and 145 pounds, play with brown belts and black belts and wrap them up like pretzels. Jiu-jitsu is where you check your ego at the door.

I had many fights as a teenager and multiple prison fights and I thought I could handle myself in Jiu-jitsu without too much trouble. This was different. In those situations you're fighting for your life and your body is going at one hundred percent for maybe a minute, if that. In Jiu-jitsu, you are learning techniques and ground fighting. You are rolling on the mats for five minutes minimum. It's exhausting but you know you are learning something that only one percent of the world population knows. Despite the exhaustion, it's a huge stress reliever. When someone is choking you, or trying to break your arm, the last thing you are thinking about is work. I also like the camaraderie: my training partners, new ones and old ones, are great guys to spend time with.

About a year into it, I did my first tournament. The biggest thing with tournaments is getting over the anxiety of events coming up before the match, but my anxiety would go away as soon as I stepped on the mat.

When I first started competing, I was having anxiety—heavy anxiety—just thinking of the tournament, which would kick in about two weeks before the tournament began. You know they're coming up, and you have to get in shape. That day was getting closer, and two weeks became one week, and it became two days, and then I was going to fight my opponent in five minutes. My stress level was high.

I wanted to do well in front of my peers, my wife, my kids, and I didn't want to embarrass myself, or my team, or my coaches. You have to tell yourself that the opponent feels the same way, and he's also nervous and anxious. But who is more anxious? You can start throwing up and cramping up, and even passing out from the anxiety. It's scary. It takes getting used to in order to continue going back to tournaments. Winning helps.

I eventually won my first match and my first gold medal, and I have continued competing to this day. I have won a dozen gold medals in Brazilian Jiu-jitsu including gold at the World Championships in Las Vegas and gold at the Pan American Games. I am not saying this to boast at all, for I have the utmost humility about my Jiu-jitsu in my life.

In 2014, I decided to compete in an international tournament. I had been training for a year and a half and just earned my blue belt. I was having a lot of fun training and wanted to test my skills. However, training for competition was a shock to my system and I mean that in a literal sense.

My first competition training pushed me into a state of panic within two seconds of beginning it. This panic was something I had never experienced, and I needed to get past it, or learn to deal with it. I can remember the anxiety leading up to my competition date. Every moment that I thought of the match, my blood pressure would increase. I wanted to compete well—win or lose. When you're competing, your coach, training partners and your family are watching. Ivette was nervous and didn't want me to compete; she was afraid I might get hurt. I can't blame her for thinking like that, but I wanted to test myself. The stress was so intense that I had even asked Ivette to book us on a cruise after the tournament so I could relax.

The day finally came to compete in that international tournament, and I won gold. What a relief that was, as once the competition was over, the stress left me. I was happy afterwards to be taking a cruise with Ivette and the girls. On May 2, 2014, we all set out on the cruise. Ivette and Nina had just gotten over the flu, and Alanna had a fever the morning we got on the ship. The following night, I felt a fever coming on after watching a comedy show with the girls. I told Ivette that I needed to go lie down.

We returned to the cabin pretty late, and I quickly fell asleep, while Ivette and the girls watched TV. Around midnight, I woke up with my heart pounding, having trouble breathing, in a cold sweat. This powerful fear came over me and I didn't know where it was coming from. Ivette saw that I was in trouble and followed me to the bathroom. Alanna and Nina were also watching me and knew that I wasn't OK.

The big point here is that though I can now call it a panic attack, we did not know at the time that this was what I was experiencing. I put cold water on my face and the panic went away. I went back to bed and fell asleep. I would wake up three more times that night in a full panic attack mode. The following days on the ship saw me gasping for breath, shaking, and full of fear, but I didn't know what anxiety felt like. I just thought that I might have the flu.

When I got off the ship a few days later, I called Nella. Being a nurse, she should know what was happening to me, I figured. When I told her, she said, "It was a panic attack, and it was time." I said, "Time for what?" "Time to see a therapist," she said. I kiddingly told her she was the one who was nuts. I mean, why would I want to talk about crap that happened twenty or thirty years ago? I was glad to be off the ship and felt fine now.

A week later, we were all at Nella's celebrating her receiving her bachelor's degree. I had one too many drinks, but I wasn't drunk. I was dancing and having a great time with the family. The following day, though, the anxiety that I felt on the cruise came back with force.

Panic attacks were now happening throughout the day and night. I couldn't sleep and I could hardly get any work done. I truly had no clue what the hell was happening to me. I became very claustrophobic: I became afraid of the dark, and I couldn't watch anything violent on TV or at the movies—and I was afraid of crowds. Also, food was going right through me, and I was losing weight. My faith in God kept me strong, but even so, I couldn't go to church because of the crowds that would surround me there.

Soon, Ivette scheduled an appointment with a doctor, and he prescribed Xanax for my anxiety. He said I needed sleep and that my serotonin levels were low. I had never taken medication, so I was reluctant, but I decided to try it for a few days. I tried it for three days and felt better so I stopped taking the prescribed Xanax. I didn't tell Ivette I had stopped the medication, and after a few days the anxiety and panic attacks came right back. It had been a month already and I still felt terrible. The nights were filled with fear, and I could hardly get any sleep. I just wanted it to end.

My doctor wanted me to come back to see him in two weeks. I did, and he said he wanted to increase the medication. I told him, "Don't tell me the name of the medication, tell my wife and she will look into it." When we got in the car, Ivette googled the medication and told me that she didn't think I should take it because of the side effects, suicidal thoughts being one of them. "Get me another doctor," I told her.

My coach, Parrumpa, called me to ask why I wasn't training. I told him I was going through something, and that I would fill him in later. I told him that no matter what, I would start training on July 1.

Meanwhile, Ivette and I went to another doctor, Angel Mesa, in West Palm Beach. Dr. Mesa asked me, "What's the problem?" I told him what had happened on the cruise, the anxiety and the panic attacks. Then he asked me, "What happened to you in the past?"

The question caught my wife and I off guard. My wife and I don't talk to just anyone about where I've been. I responded back, "Why do you ask?"

He said, "You have PTSD. It is set off by something that happened to you in the past, so what is it?"

I thought to myself, I haven't been here two seconds and he's telling me I have PTSD. I asked him a second question, "How do you know I have PTSD"?

He answered, "Because I had it."

Dr. Mesa pulled down his shirt collar, showing me his trachea scar. He said he had been in a car accident and was paralyzed from the neck down for six months, which caused him to have PTSD. "You have my same symptoms," Dr. Mesa said to me, "and you need to see a psychiatrist right away."

I felt fifty percent better just knowing I had a diagnosis. My wife still thought I had something else, maybe a stomach virus since my stomach was still very bad. But Dr. Mesa said, "No flu or stomach virus here."

This is what www.psychiatry.org says about PTSD:

Posttraumatic stress disorder (PTSD) is a psychiatric disorder that may occur in people who have experienced or witnessed a traumatic event, series of events or set of circumstances. An individual may experience this as emotionally or physically harmful or life-threatening and may affect mental, physical, social, and/or spiritual well-being. Examples include natural disasters, serious accidents, terrorist acts, war/combat, rape/sexual assault, historical trauma,

> *intimate partner violence and bullying. PTSD has been known by many names in the past, such as "shell shock" during the years of World War I and "combat fatigue" after World War II, but PTSD does not just happen to combat veterans. PTSD can occur in all people, of any ethnicity, nationality or culture, and at any age...*

Ivette and I left relieved that we had a diagnosis and were now searching for a way to move forward with my healing. Friends of ours, Lidia and Angel Borges, whom we had met in a Bible study group years earlier and who remain very close to this day, knew what I was going through. They recommended a Christian therapist.

I scheduled a meeting with Dr. John Hawkins at Gateway Counseling in Boynton Beach. He is a kind, gentle and soft-spoken man and I felt right at ease—as much as I could. In our first meeting, I told him what was happening, and he asked me to write down on a piece of paper any traumatic events from my past so we could review them. I took the sheet and began writing. I filled the page on the front, and then the flip side of it. I had a lot of trauma to reveal.

When John looked at my sheet, he told me that his clients would generally describe one traumatic event. I had just filled the front and back page with traumatic events. I wrote down the multiple home invasions, the murders of my mother and Kiko, the shootings, my time in prison, my father's murder, and my weeks and months of time spent in solitary confinement. I said, "Yeah, it's a lot for a lifetime".

I also told him I had changed my life and that I had left my "old" life behind a long time ago. Now I needed to deal with this "old" life because it was very much present, and I asked him if he could help me. He said to follow his instructions and that I would feel eighty percent better in approximately eight weeks.

John then gave me several assignments and told me to continue training in Jiu-jitsu: it would be good for me as I made a journey back to every place I had felt fear. He said I needed to expose myself to all my fears and that, gradually, the intensity of my PTSD would decline through this exposure.

A few weeks later, John asked me to write a letter to my father. I knew I had to find the path of forgiveness to start to let things go. Not only did I have to forgive my father, but I had to forgive my mother as well. Both my parents had made choices that put themselves, and my sister and me, in terrible situations. That's actually an understatement.

By now, this PTSD literally had me on my knees. All the traumatic events in my life had happened around me, but PTSD was happening to my mind. What I was feeling was very dark, and only God Himself could help me through this. If it took releasing all the hatred I had built up over the past thirty years, then that is what I would have to do to be done with it.

My therapist Dr. John advised me to write a letter to my father for closure. I wrote the letter to my father. It took me weeks to sit down and do it, but I finally released it all to God.

Ovidio,

Where do I begin? I guess describing to you all that I know about you so you can see what type of man you were while on this earth.

You were a liar, an abuser of all types (women, children & alcohol). You abused women verbally and physically, children, you abused me physically, and after what happened with Lina, I believe you abused her sexually as well.

Lina was 12. I can't comprehend how you were not even embarrassed for us when Doris came to us with your love letters to a 12-year-old girl. My daughter is 12 and if I had found letters like that in my daughter's possession, our lives would have been much different, but it's amazing you got away with it.

You got away with the murder of my mother, Bianella's mother, and our uncle and who knows how many more are underground. Because of your beliefs that a person could not make a penny in this country I followed in your footsteps and got involved selling drugs. Thanks to your mentorship I spent almost 11 years in a Federal prison.

You are the exact definition of the scum of the earth, of how not to be a father, husband, businessman or friend. I don't know what could've happened in your life that made you into what you became. It doesn't make a difference anymore.

I can tell you now that I am the total opposite of the man you were. I am a great father. I tell my kids I love them, where you never said those words to me. If I remember correctly, you said you didn't love me when I was 16.

I live a legitimate life with no fear of anyone robbing me or trying to hurt my family. I believe I've become a good husband, though I didn't start out like one. I've never beat my wife or kids.

Bianella and myself chose to break those chains that many people continue to walk the same footsteps their parents did.

Ovidio, because of every traumatic moment in my life you have had a hand in, and now I am dealing with the emotional effects of all of it. Which has been much worse than the beatings, my mother and Kiko's murder including my imprisonment. These last 3 to 4 months have been harder than everything combined.

I can tell you that if it weren't for Jesus Christ I don't think I would be here now writing you this letter. He has relieved me from the anger that I felt for so many many years.

> *It is because of this that I have the strength to forgive you for all of your cruelties. I forgive you for the beatings, for the murders of my mother and uncle, I forgive you for "everything".*
>
> *I release you to God, Jesus Christ.*

I had to now see my father as a boy, and thought how his father would still love him knowing all he did. I thought of my daughters, asking myself if there was anything they could do that would stop me from loving them? And I knew the answer. God still loved my father and probably waited for my father to come back to Him, but he never did. My father will remain in hell, and that is a place I am not going to go to with him.

I don't know where my mother is, but I hope and pray she is in a better place. My mother had some faith in God, but she also dabbled in Santeria, Tarot cards and psychic mediums. The Bible is pretty clear on what we should stay away from. So I chose to forgive "EVERYONE" and be grateful for everything I had. I was grateful to God for sending me to prison, for bringing Ivette to me, for my children, for taking care of my sister Nella while I was away, for my half-sisters who were innocent in all this, for my career, for my physical health, for all the prayers directed at me, and I was now even grateful for my PTSD which had brought me to this point PTSD changed me: it humbled me. I feel it made me a better man for my wife and kids. Since my release in 2000, I was not always with God. There were a few times in which I turned my back on Him and I know now that, although I wasn't always with God, God was always with me. I now have a personal relationship with God and thank Him for the blessings in my life, my marriage, my children, and my businesses. I give all glory to God for everything, and I can tell you this, my fear and love of God continues to grow day by day as I see how beautiful life can be. I have seen and experienced the worst but have also seen what God can do for you as well. I owe everything to Him.

I kept seeing Dr. John Hawkins for those eight weeks, which did make me better, but I continued seeing him for another year just to be sure I had all the tools I needed to move forward. Besides seeing Dr. John, I continued training and did cold water therapy and breathing techniques. I believe the combination of everything helped me get out of the hole I was in and to celebrate my greatest accomplishment, my family. I have come back as a husband, a father and a Jiu-jitsu champion, and it all started in that cell in solitary confinement more than thirty years ago. Asking God for help was the best choice I ever made. It's hard sometimes to see His work, but my favorite verse in the Bible is "It came to pass." This verse is said four hundred and fifty-two times in the Bible. And for me it did just that, "and it came to pass."

Today, I am part of the Kairos Ministry Group. Kairos preaches to inmates across the United States, and I am part of a small group in Palm Beach County. My brother-in-law, Eric, invited me to the group and I am grateful to him for the invitation. Our group comes together several times a year and works to bring inmates to God. It's the least I can do in response to all that He has done for me.

CHAPTER 10: Healing the Mind

Nella speaks...

When my brother went through PTSD, that was the scariest time. I would never in a million years have ever thought that I would see him like that. He was in a very dark place.

I thought maybe he had cancer because of his extreme weight loss, but then he finally told me he had PTSD. I didn't know enough about PTSD at the time, but I knew he was having a terrible time. He decided to rent a house in Naples and invited us over. We were in the house he had rented, and we were talking in the kitchen. I told him that I thought his anxiety had to do with our mother, and her murder. He agreed and felt it was part of it.

I told him to continue going to therapy and spoke of my experience with therapy. I said my therapist thought the reason that I spoke about my mother to everyone was because I was creating witnesses to make it real for me. I needed to make it real for myself.

When I said that, he broke down and started crying. It was like the proverbial floodgates had opened, and he just lay sobbing on my lap. And he cried and cried and cried. I told him, "It's okay, you need to let it out." Then he sat up, took a breath of fresh air, and told me that he felt so good. He had never cried for our mother, and I knew that there would be a lot more tears coming.

He went to his therapist, who gave him homework. He had to write a letter to our father. And he did.

CHAPTER 11: Healing The Soul

Nella on faith…
My mother was very influential with my faith. My memories of her lighting a candle and praying at night are very vivid. But so are the other memories of her belief in the occult world. Fortune tellers, mediums and psychics were also part of her beliefs. This in turn led me to be curious about other beliefs during my years in college. I ultimately found comfort and peace in the Bible. I like the smell of incense, the sound of church bells ringing, and the love of Christ. I believe in the Holy Trinity and I honor the Blessed Virgin Mary. I believe in a great and loving God who sent his son Jesus to be our Savior. He is the great "I am."

I recall sharing my concerns with my father before he died. I told him that it was not acceptable to take someone's life. I told him that I worried about his spirit when he died.

He responded, "On Earth, money and power rule and when my time is up, I will be in the great God's mercy."

If my dreams have any meaning, then he has seen the sorrows and intense sufferings he caused to so many. As my final and most difficult act of faith, I learned with the help of the Holy Spirit and therapy to release him by granting him forgiveness. For as long as I did not forgive, I remained his prisoner. I am happy to say that I am free of him. I am at peace. I feel joy, happiness and love every day of my life.

Do I want to find the people who killed my mother and uncle? No. I am afraid of retaliation. And I tell my brother, we have to think of our family, our children. I want protection. Not everyone can forgive and forget what happened thirty or forty years ago. You can't assume that people are as forgiving as we are. You can't assume to know where people are spiritually and mentally. I would not want somebody to come and kill my children and make them pay for my father's mistakes. You know, it dies with them. It died with my mother and it died with my father. It was their choices that led them to this, and we were victims of it. We did not want to become victims, but we did want to learn from our experience and grow from it.

And to this day, I'm still struggling. My kids are always wanting to go back to Colombia, and it's such a beautiful culture and a beautiful country. I am reluctant to go. I still have that fear. While my brother was in jail, I kept going to Colombia to visit my dad until 1998 when he died. I saw the car he was killed in. I saw his blood. And I have seen what people can do out of anger and revenge. No more.

I live in love. Today, Tony and I remain more in love than ever. "Oh my Tony! Love of my life! Light of my eyes!" – is what I still say to him. Imagine, I'm in love with my best friend, husband, and soulmate. A true gift from God. He has never abandoned me. He gives me the love and the support to be myself. I married him and his wonderful loving family. I can see the hand of God giving me back what I lost, but in a way I would not have imagined. We have three beautiful and loving kids. We became a family and created a happy home. My prayer was answered.

Alain on faith...

On Thanksgiving 2022, my brother-in-law Eric told me that he had gone to do ministry at the Okeechobee Correctional Institution, which is a state prison for men located in Okeechobee County, Florida, about a two-and-a-half-hour drive north from Miami. The facility has a mix of security levels, including minimum, medium, and close, and the prison houses over sixteen hundred adult males.

When Eric went to OCI, he was acting out of Christian charity: he had never been incarcerated. When he told me about his visit to OCI, I told him that I had always wanted to do something like that. Indeed, I had been praying for the opportunity to do something like that for God—and for the prisoners.

The next ministry was going to take place in May, and he invited me to join them in it. I said a resounding "Yes!" and we prepared for nine weeks by taking classes about what we wanted to present to the prisoners and what we wanted to accomplish in our time with them. And then I did my first ministry in OCI.

The session takes four days, and we stayed in a hotel because we have to begin each day at 7 am.

We set up six tables in the Chapel, and there were nine guys at each table, three of us plus six inmates. We fed them breakfast and lunch, and the food was good. They enjoyed steak, ribs and muffins. This is all made possible thanks to the donations that covered the food.

We do some singing. We do a lot of praying. We have a curriculum that we have to follow: it was designed by psychologists to gradually break down the prisoners and allow them to hear the word of God. By the third or fourth day, they're all humbled and grateful for our kindness.

I didn't tell the inmates at my table that I had also been in prison. But they asked me if I would be part of the group who would give testimony, part of the group that speaks out about their lives. Kairos already had me scheduled to do so last, and I said, "Yes, I will be giving my testimony on the final day."

I had become really friendly with these guys, and they were very eager to hear my story, of which they knew nothing. They said that my story must be really good if they were having me speak last, because that's the point when they usually have an inmate speak. But this time it was me.

On the last day, it was time to give my testimony. I told them a summary about my life and I found myself getting emotional while I was telling my story.

When I finished, everybody stood up, and they were all applauding. All the guys at my table surrounded me and hugged me. Some got emotional. I held back my tears. It was just a real emotional moment.

I finally got out of the Chapel and went into the library, and then in the company of three of my guys from the ministry, and four inmates, I broke down and cried like a baby. They all began praying over me, thanking me for my testimony and thanking me for coming. Some told me that their story was very similar to mine. I don't want to reveal anything that was said to me in confidence but let me say that there were people in the prison to whom I could very much relate.

I was uneasy about the applause that I received for my testimony. When I finally saw Eric, he said I had given a hell of a testimony. That everybody said it was great. But to me it was brutal. I felt guilty that I had received that applause for something that happened in my life that was a torture to me.

Then I finally understood that they were applauding me and hugging me and yelling for me, because of what God had done in my life to help me heal the torture. They wanted the same thing. They saw how I had spent ten years in prison and survived it. I had emerged into a full and rewarding life. I had gone forward, sometimes uphill, sometimes down, but always forward. I'm not a perfect Christian. But I try my damnedest. I try to always keep my eyes on God because I know that God is watching me, and now He is helping me to help others who are living what I once lived.

Alain's favorite Bible verses

These are some Bible verses which I, Alain, have found helpful to me on my journey. All quotes taken from the ERV version of the Bible at https://www.biblegateway.com/.

> *And if my people who are called by my name become humble and pray, and look for me, and turn away from their evil ways, then I will hear them from heaven. I will forgive their sin and heal their land.*
>
> 2 Chronicles 7:14

> *Christ is the one who gives me the strength I need to do whatever I must do.*
>
> Philippians 4:13

> *Don't worry—I am with you.*
> *Don't be afraid—I am your God.*
> *I will make you strong and help you.*
> *I will support you with my right hand that brings victory.*
>
> Isaiah 41:10

"I say this because I know the plans that I have for you." This message is from the Lord. "I have *good plans for you. I don't plan to hurt you. I plan to give you hope and a good future."*

Jeremiah 29:11

We know that in everything God works for the good of those who love him. These are the people God chose, because that was his plan.

Romans 8:28

When Jesus heard this, he said to them, "It is the sick people who need a doctor, not those who are healthy. I did not come to invite good people. I came to invite sinners."

Mark 2:17

Be strong and be brave. Don't be afraid of those people because the Lord your God is with you. He will not fail you or leave you.

Deuteronomy 31:6

Lord, you are my Light and my Savior, so why would I be afraid of anyone? The Lord is where my life is safe, so I will be afraid of no one!

Psalms 27:1

It is yours because when I was hungry, you gave me food to eat. When I was thirsty, you gave me something to drink. When I had no place to stay, you welcomed me into your home. When I was without clothes, you gave me something to wear. When I was sick, you cared for me. When I was in prison, you came to visit me.

Matthew 25: 35-36

Yes, God loved the world so much that he gave his only Son, so that everyone who believes in him would not be lost but have eternal life.

John 3:16

Florida, 1990: Nella graduating from college with her Fairy Godmother Lupe.

1998: Nella graduating from Nursing School, Miami Dade College, pregnant with Isa.

May 30, 1998: Nella and Tony under a happy storm of wedding confetti: Nonna is on the right.

Florida, 2000: One hour after Alain got out of prison, with Ivette.

2000: Nella with her Fairy Godmother Thelma.

Florida, 2000: Ivette and Alain share a kiss on the beach in front of Nella's home.

Florida, August 2001: Alain and Ivette's engagement party. From left to right: Ivette, Alain, Nella and Tony.

2023: Nella with her Fairy Godmother Lupe.

2017: Nella at the Baptist Hospital, Miami, receiving her Daisy Award in honor of extraordinary nursing, alongside husband Tony, son Dassio, and daughters Isa and Bianella.

August 2001: Alain and Ivette on their wedding day at Vizcaya, the historic mansion in Miami, Florida.

Florida, August 2001: Nella and Tony at Alain and Ivette's wedding.

Miami Marathon 1991: Nella's first marathon.

2024: Nella (609) and daughter Isa (608) run the Miami Marathon.

2024: Alain with his brown belt in Brazilian Jiu-Jitsu and 12 gold medals, with his coach and trainer Marcos "Parrumpa" DaMatta.

2023: Family Birthday. From right to left: Nella, our son and middle child Dassio, Isa the eldest, Tony, and Bianella, the youngest.

2023: At a wedding, Alain and Ivette with daughters Nina and Alanna.

Florida, Christmas 2007: Nella, Nonna Edith, Nonno Roberto, Lorena.

Florida, 2025: Nonna, Nella, Lorena.

2024: Nella and Alain.

Acknowledgements

I am deeply grateful to Michael McKinley and Nancy Bell for their patience and invaluable guidance in writing our story. The compassion and desire to help us share our story to help others has been a driving force. Thank you for listening to us for so many hours which very much felt like therapy.

To Nonna, Lupe and Thelma, my fairy Godmothers: May God bless you infinitely for providing the Love I need in my mother's absence. Each of you filled a role that made all the difference in my life.

To Nonna and Nonno: You took me into your home and fed me not only good food but also the love and the warmth of a peaceful home. You gave me Lore, my sister and soulmate. I felt the love of a father with Nonno as he always introduced me as his "other daughter."

To Lupita mi Corazon: Thank you for opening the doors to your home as well and feeding me Italian food, tea and toast in the morning as we got ready for work and your endless most heartwarming hugs. You shared your family with me, and I found a sister in Jean, a heart of gold with nothing but kindness in her heart. Her friendship is a gift I will always treasure in my heart.

To Thelma: How can I ever thank you enough? You were the first person to say I was smart; you believed in me. You gave me books to read and encouraged me to discover my potential. I learned to water ski by your side and ran a marathon by your side. You made it possible for me to live my dream of becoming a nurse. Thank you for paying for my education and my livelihood when I needed it the most. I will always be your petunia.

To my light posts: The following individuals were also put in my life by God, showing me the way on my journey: Dr. Dimino, I babysat his 3 children and learned so much about raising children. His wife and family educated me and without knowing it, the little girl in me grew up to watching Disney movies for the first time as I babysat.

Dr. Robert Salzman and Dr. Anthony Albanese: Wow! These men were so kind and noble, and truly inspiring. I'm grateful they believed in me, Dr. Salzman knew my history and welcomed me into his office and treated me like family. If it wasn't for him I would not be in Baptist Hospital. Dr. Albanese, a true follower of Christ, he prayed with me and for me; he took me to church, and he stood up for me. In my 20s, Dr. Albanese made a deep impact in my life. A true and loving husband and father, I remember he would spend weekends with church youth group while working full-time in internal medicine, and then went on to open a center to help those who suffer from addictions.

Thank you to Renee Nathan, who opened the doors for me when I needed it the most. To Dr. Pablo Delgado who taught me so much in the Labor Room. I am a better nurse because of the time he took to teach me. He shared his intelligence and his fatherly heart with me . It was a privilege to be loved by him. To my Labor room family! Patty, Elba, Tracey, Jamee, Kristy, Yanet, Elena, Angela, Acklin, Ivette, Nicole, Marcela, Janet, Carol, Clarisse, Natalie, Bethann, Cassandra, Raquel, Jean, Lizzie and Kelly are among so many more who together have witnessed life and death, as well as the historical event of the pandemic. Each of you holds a very special place in my heart.

We share our vulnerabilities as we navigate life together as women helping others while trying our best to be good nurses, wives, moms, daughters and friends. We hold each other up and are always there in time of need.

To Jessica Aviles, my dear friend who brought me closer to God and whose loving friendship I will always cherish. I am a better person because of you.

To my sisters who inspired me to be better and to be the anchor in our family.

To my Nana, Vivi and Edwin, the De la Hoz family: all of you welcomed me into your family and I am proud to hold your name. I love you each of you so much.

To Ivette who has stood by my brother's side in the toughest of times and has always been his love. Thank you for the love and support you give him daily for his happiness and wellbeing. May God Forever Bless You.

To my dear brother, Alain: how I love you. You have always shown resilience and strength when faced with adversity. You managed to smile in the saddest times and in turn inspire me to smile too. You inspired me to keep moving forward as you were imprisoned and I was determined to show you a new path. I wanted you to see a life of righteousness and success. I thank God for making it true. I am proud of the good you choose to do each day and for choosing to honor God. Mami is no doubt very proud. I must thank you as well for the advice you gave me as a young girl: "Nella, don't ever give someone else the power to choose if they want you… If they have doubt... You choose you and walk away."

To my other soulmate sister, Lore: My Life is more beautiful because of you. Thank you for inspiring me to be a better version of self since we met in 1984. You inspired me to study, be disciplined, exercise, read, learn etiquette, the arts, culture, traveling. Then learning how to be the wives we aspired to be, the mothers we wished to become and the incredible women we are. I love seeing how excited you get to see me happy or achieving anything. I love how you council our kiddos, how Tony calls you, I love that you are the first phone call of my day. I love you, Lore, my sister, my joy.

And now to the love of my life, Anthony Dean DeLaHoz: Thank you for choosing to walk by my side with your unfailing love and support. I can always count on you for anything. You make me laugh; you bring me peace. Together we have raised three kind, loving souls and have been our greatest joy in life. Being your wife and mother to our children has been my greatest honor.

Isabella, Dassio and Biani: Thank you for being so kind and compassionate with us. Being your Mom is my greatest happiness. In each of you I see the best of Papi and I.

With my family I see God's Promise come true.

~ Nella

Alain's Acknowledgements...

After giving my testimony at OCI for Kairos ministry, I decided it was time to finally write this book. For many years, I was ashamed of the life I led so long ago. Today I'm more proud of and grateful for the life God has provided me. I'm grateful to my wife Ivette, for making the decision in 1993 to visit me in prison: had she not done so, God only knows where I would have ended up. If it weren't for her I may have made the wrong decision and gone back to Colombia in 1995 after speaking with Marco. I truly believe I might not be alive today if it weren't for Ivette coming into my life. She has given me two beautiful daughters that have grown into beautiful human beings. I Thank her for loving me unconditionally over the last three decades. I thank Ivette and thank God for the gift of love.

To Alanna and Nina, I'm grateful to you girls for showing what love for a child feels like, and inspiring me every day to be a great and proud father.

I'm grateful for my sister Nella, for this journey we made together throughout these last fifty-plus years. I can't imagine getting through the first half of our lives without each other. I'm so proud of the beautiful person she has become.

I'm grateful to Tony for our friendship over the last forty years, and for sticking by me. I am grateful to KC for our conversations and putting me on my career path. And I'm grateful to Accredited Appraisal Associates for hiring and training me in 2001. I thank God for using everyone in my life who has helped me and made me the man I am today. I want to thank my wife again most importantly for hanging in there through all the craziness. I owe you my life. I love you, babe!

And to those reading this memoir, I want to say this. If you find yourself in a dark place, I'm here to tell you it will come to pass. I look forward to going back into the prisons, to telling the men inside them that I too have been where they are. I show them that, yes, there is a way out if you follow the word of the Lord. My wish for you in reading this story is that you will take away its message of hope and its power to heal.

You will have seen in our story that while we can experience the worst of life, we can, in turn, make the best of life. That is my wish for you all. To live well, and to do good.

God Bless You All!

-Alain

The Authors

Bianella Orozco-DeLaHoz was born in Brooklyn, New York. She earned her Bachelor of Science from Miami Dade College and is nationally certified as an expert Inpatient Obstetric Nurse. She has worked as a Labor and Delivery nurse for over 25 years at Baptist Hospital of Miami. A three-time marathon runner and proud mother of three, Bianella considers her greatest accomplishment to be the loving family she built with the love of her life, Anthony.

Bianella shares her story to inspire those who have suffered loss and trauma to embark on a path of healing and joy. Choosing to know and love God has been her constant source of strength and grace. Her journey from tragedy to healing is rooted in her unwavering faith in Jesus, who illuminated her path with beacons of hope: her devoted husband, lifelong friends, Godmothers and mentors who helped her rebuild her life. She hopes you allow God into your heart and let him show you the way.

Alain Orozco was born in Brooklyn, New York, alongside his twin sister Bianella. His early life was shaped by hardship. After relocating to Florida, he faced the harsh realities of growing up with a father involved in drug dealing. Though that path led Alain to spend over a decade in federal prison on drug-related charges, it was there where he began his path to redemption.

Upon his release, Alain rebuilt his life from the ground up, becoming a Certified Residential Property Appraiser, a career he's pursued for more than 24 years. Working from home gave him the priceless opportunity to be present for his wife of 24 years and raise their two daughters, a role he cherishes above all.

Alain's discipline extends beyond business. He's a Black Belt in Brazilian Jiu-Jitsu and 12-time IBJJF Champion, and trains regularly at American Top Team, proving that strength isn't just physical—it's mental, emotional, and spiritual. Today, Alain resides in West Palm Beach, Florida, where he continues his business in Appraising Real Estate, building homes, training in Jiu Jitsu, and living with purpose. His journey is a testament to the power of redemption, resilience, and relentless determination.

www.ingramcontent.com/pod-product-compliance
Lightning Source LLC
Chambersburg PA
CBHW050526100526
44581CB00008B/144/J